# SISTER CARRIE

## NOTES

*including*
- *Life of Dreiser*
- *Critical Introduction*
- *Brief Synopsis of the Novel*
- *List of Characters*
- *Chapter Summaries and Commentaries*
- *Character Analyses*
- *Dreiser's Ideas and Philosophy*
- *Notes on Symbolism, Style, and Chapter Titles*
- *Review Questions and Theme Topics*
- *Selected Bibliography*

*by*
Frederick J. Balling, M.A.

D1411691

INCORPORATED

LINCOLN, NEBRASKA 68501

Editor

Gary Carey, M.A.
University of Colorado

Consulting Editor

James L. Roberts, Ph.D.
Department of English
University of Nebraska

ISBN 0-8220-1201-4
© Copyright 1967
by
Cliffs Notes, Inc.
All Rights Reserved
Printed in U.S.A.

1998 Printing

The Cliffs Notes logo, the names "Cliffs" and "Cliffs Notes," and the black and yellow diagonal-stripe cover design are all registered trademarks belonging to Cliffs Notes, Inc., and may not be used in whole or in part without written permission.

Cliffs Notes, Inc.          Lincoln, Nebraska

# CONTENTS

# Sister Carrie Notes

## LIFE OF DREISER

Born August 27, 1871, Theodore Dreiser was the second youngest of a family of ten children. Dreiser's father had come from Germany twenty-five years before and through hard work became a man of wealth and position. Just before Theodore's birth, a series of misfortunes had struck the family, rendering them penniless. John Paul Dreiser, the father, was crippled shortly after his weaving mill had burned down. While he convalesced, his wife was cheated out of the remainder of the family property by creditors. The elder Dreiser was unable to secure employment to support his large family. Always a devout and orthodox Roman Catholic, he grew increasingly fanatical in his concern for salvation. Forever on guard to preserve the virtue of his children and to pay off his debts lest he die owing money, he became an unbearable despot and led the family into near beggary. Even as an infant, Theodore learned the difficult lessons of poverty, chance, and morality.

Dreiser's mother, in contrast to the stern religious fanaticism of the father, was full of tender sentiment and not subject to his adamant morality. Quiet by nature, sympathetic and gentle, she was nonetheless endowed with endless strength and patience. Sarah Dreiser was eager to be helpful and stood by to aid any child with whom the father was angry.

The father's religious fanaticism, the mother's abiding tenderness, and the family's unbearable poverty worked together in shaping the young Dreiser. As a product of these conditions, Dreiser was possessed of a furious energy, a determination to succeed, and an unalterable will.

In 1879 it was decided that the family should split up. The three youngest children, including Theodore, went with the mother. Free now from the stern wrath of his father, Theodore roamed the open fields and played along the waterways and streams of Evansville, Indiana. He learned much from nature, perceiving in it many analogies to human life. Passenger trains heading for Santa Fe, San Francisco, Denver, and Chicago fired his imagination of faraway places. The boy dreamed especially of Chicago, the magic city where young men and women of the Midwest sought their fortunes.

Appearing after a four-year absence, dressed in silk hat and fur coat, the oldest brother Paul, now a successful song writer, returned to lift the family out of its poverty. In the figure of Paul, Theodore found a concept of fortune in the affairs of men. The strangest of coincidence seemed to him to be the origin of a powerful, arbitrary, interfering fate. The concept of fate finds expression throughout all of Dreiser's novels, in which the loosest of coincidences play a decisive role in human existence.

Although he was a poor grammar student and barely passed in his studies, Dreiser read widely in the classics. His teacher was able to convince him, however, that he was worth something despite his own harsh judgment of himself. At the age of sixteen Dreiser announced to his mother that he was going to Chicago. With the six dollars that she gave him, he took his first steps on the long way to fame and fortune.

After innumerable setbacks and disappointments, he eventually found work in a hardware store. Working closely with the sons of wealthy Eastern executives, he came to hate the disparity between their wealth and his poverty. Out of the comparison of his own lot with that of those more fortunate, he came to see for himself how life was organized. Through contrast of affluence and poverty, Dreiser thought, individuals come to enjoy or disdain what they possess or do not possess.

Through a stroke of fortune, which he believed to be fate itself, Dreiser was given money by his former schoolteacher to attend Indiana University. For the first time in his life he felt important. But the university did not offer the opportunities for learning he had so much hoped for. Life itself was destined to be Dreiser's college. Books were of some value to him but they would never supplant the direct observations of the human struggle that the adolescent Dreiser was already used to. The university only confirmed his notion that success in life came with luck and money and good clothes. He left the university after his freshman year.

Determined to rise above the struggles of the poor, he moved from job to job until he eventually found trial employment with the *Daily Globe*, Chicago's smallest newspaper. For the next decade he was occupied solely with the work of journalism. He worked as a reporter and editor and wrote scores of feature articles for popular magazines. Journalism offered nothing to change his ideas of life's vicissitudes; it merely reinforced them and gave them shape. He gathered up experience in the "grim, fierce struggle of life," and although he felt no identification with the oppressed, his sympathy lay with the underdog.

Throughout the ten years of his newspaper career Dreiser was continually and forcefully struck by the severe contrast between the truth in life as he saw it daily and the illusion of actual life he was required to present in his articles. Dreiser was invited to New York by his elder brother Paul and decided to go. Perhaps there, Dreiser thought, a man could write the truth and still find success.

He wandered about for five months — Toledo, Cleveland, Buffalo, Pittsburgh — before finally arriving in New York. Much of the panorama of American life in a greatly formative era had passed before his observant eyes.

Finally obtaining a reporting job that sometimes did not even pay for his carfare, Dreiser combed every corner of the city for news. He roamed the East Side, the Bowery, the waterfronts of Brooklyn, Wall Street, and Fifth Avenue. Human survival seemed far more difficult in New York than it was in Chicago or the steel centers of the North. Everywhere he turned he saw in humanity an overwhelming desire for pleasure or wealth, along with a heartlessness which destroyed the soul òr caused it to freeze over with misery and deprivation.

It is not surprising that at the time Dreiser read heavily in Balzac, Hardy, and Tolstoy, writers whose views complemented his own. He began to think of becoming a short story writer. Dreiser's overwhelming desire was to record his observations and conclusions about life, not as they had been distorted to fit the requirements of newspaper reporting but as he felt them to be. His first story to be published, "The Shining Slave Makers," presented a portrait of a jungle world where two rival ant colonies meet for a gruesome combat to the death.

A friend of Dreiser's, Arthur Henry, persuaded him to try his hand at a novel. Reluctantly, in the autumn of 1900 Dreiser sat down and wrote at random the title—*Sister Carrie*. It is said that Dreiser had no conception of the plot of the novel when he began to write, but soon after recalling the tragedies of his youth —the injustices which he had seen chance, ignorance, and passion play upon those whom he had known firsthand—he began to write furiously. In the novel are found the wealth of details and the range of ideas which wide experience had brought to him. In this first novel Dreiser succeeded in pointing out the tragic possibilities inherent in the conflict between the individual and a society characterized by narrow and repressive convention on the one hand and the deification of material success on the other.

Despondent and embittered by the poor reception of *Sister Carrie*, Dreiser contemplated suicide until he was once again rescued by his brother Paul, who got him a job as a magazine editor. Dreiser succeeded so well in this position that he became head of the firm in a few years. Encouraged in his writing by Paul and a few discerning critics, Dreiser published *Jennie Gerhardt* in 1911. Like *Sister Carrie*, it is a sympathetic portrait of a "sinful" woman, yet it met with a much better reception than did the first novel and Dreiser began to acquire the reputation he justly deserved.

In 1912 *The Financier* was published, the first of a "trilogy of desire" concerning the life of Frank Cowperwood, a character, who like many of Dreiser's characters, was based upon an actual person. *The Titan*, second in the trilogy (1914), shows Cowperwood as a superman who clawed his way upward from poverty to wealth and position. Both novels were very well documented in the tradition of literary naturalism, which was Dreiser's hallmark.

*The Genius* (1915) centers upon another superman, Eugene Witla, an artist who was the fictional combination of Dreiser himself, along with an artist who fascinated him and a bright young editor who committed suicide. Dreiser's next novel to appear was *An American Tragedy* (1925), based upon the notorious Chester Gillette-Grace Brown murder case of 1906. Not only Clyde Griffiths, the man who is convicted for the murder of his pregnant mistress, but society as well is held responsible for the tragedy. The society has erred in fascinating Griffiths with its glitter and wealth without providing him with a background of moral restraint. By suggesting the possibility of social reform, *An American Tragedy* seems to be less pessimistic than Dreiser's earlier works with their pervading sense of purposelessness.

Rejecting his own early fatalism, Dreiser eventually turned to socialism as a way of answering the needs of the people. Two books, *Dreiser Looks at Russia* (1928) and *Tragic America* (1931), express his faith in socialist reform.

Theodore Dreiser died of a heart attack in December, 1945. Two novels were published after his death. *The Bulwark* (1946) is an awkward story patched together over a period of thirty-six years. Its hero, Solon Barnes, a Quaker, suffers through an oversimplified view of life, for he has divided the world into good and evil. Solon learns that the world is so corrupt that no compromise between idealism and materialism is possible. *The Stoic* (1947), last of the Cowperwood trilogy, suffers because by the time it was completed Dreiser had abandoned the attitudes which hold together the first two parts. This novel presents a discussion of Oriental philosophy, which Dreiser studied seriously for some time before his death. In the leap to "pure Spirit" Dreiser seems to have found for himself a method of transcending the purposeless wandering of the materialistic flux.

Dreiser's theories of art and philosophy of life are set down at length in his nonfictional autobiographical works: *A Traveler at Forty* (1913), *A Hoosier Holiday* (1916), *A Book About Myself* (1922) (later published as *Newspaper Days*), and especially *Hey-Rub-a-Dub-Dub: A Book of the Mystery and Terror and Wonder of Life* (1920). By the time of his death the tide of naturalism had turned and Dreiser's popularity had waned substantially.

## CRITICAL INTRODUCTION

*Sister Carrie,* Dreiser's first novel, was presented to a reading public not yet ready for its stark realism and pessimistic view of life. The manuscript had already been refused by two publishers when Frank Norris, author of the powerful naturalistic novel *McTeague,* and also an editor for Doubleday, Page and Company, read the manuscript and proclaimed it to be one of the best novels he had ever read. Walter Page, a partner in the firm, joined Norris in his praise of *Sister Carrie* and signed an agreement with Dreiser to publish it. Then, Frank Doubleday, the senior partner, upon returning from Europe, read the proof sheets and stopped publication.

It was not only Doubleday's dislike of the novel, but also his business acumen which prompted him to halt publication. He knew that any novel full of such vulgarity and moral laxity would not sell. Dreiser insisted that the publisher abide by the contract, and so a thousand copies were run off and bound. The book was displayed in the wholesale showroom and listed in the company's catalog. Through Norris' intervention, over four hundred copies were sent out to reviewers. When orders came in they were promptly filled. There is no foundation to Dreiser's charge that it was "suppressed" or "buried away in a cellar." Nevertheless, it is fair to say that the book, through Doubleday's influence, received the very minimum of publicity.

Favorable reviews were very few. Most reviewers were violently adverse and insulting. *Sister Carrie* was labeled immoral and vulgar. The book-purchasing public had no quarrel with the reviewers. Dreiser had much faith both in the book and the public. He bought the printing plates of his own novel and had it republished in successively larger editions in 1907, 1908, 1911, and 1932. Dreiser had finally triumphed over the genteel literary tradition.

Judged by the stiff-necked moral and esthetic standards of 1900, *Sister Carrie* was a shocking book. In *McTeague*, the most daring novel of the times, lust and vice were punished in the end to furnish the reader with a moral lesson. Carrie, far from being punished, involves herself compromisingly with two men and winds up in luxury, a successful actress, "with glory ringing in her ears" as she collects an enormous salary—a denouement that could be interpreted as advocating an unchaste life.

In addition to this, the novel may have offended public taste for any of the following reasons: It presented uneducated people who spoke ungrammatically and colloquially; it was vulgar. Dreiser compounds his offenses by showing sympathy for such vulgar characters in their sordid entanglements. All of its characters were "adrift on a storm sea," unable to steer any course, able only to grasp whatever comfort was washed their way. This violated the current moral doctrine of progress and free will, which taught that every man could choose his own ways of good or evil. The pessimism of *Sister Carrie* offended the contemporary taste for sweetness.

Walter Page wrote to Dreiser that, although his workmanship was "excellent," his choice of characters was "unfortunate." He feared that *Sister Carrie* would corrupt the public.

*Sister Carrie* was in fact a book so far ahead of its time that it is as alive and valid today as when it was written. Beyond that, it allows the present-day reader to enter into the consciousness of an era that is no more. Dreiser's talent lies in his ability to present life as he saw it, raw and ungrammatical, unpolished and tragic. Dreiser saw his role as a craftsman of detail, not of words or style.

Reminiscing over the novel he once wrote: "It is not intended as a piece of literary craftsmanship, but as a picture of conditions done as simple and effectively as the English language will permit." (See notes on Style.) It is through an overwhelming mass of detail — of clothing, manners, speech, actual news items — that Dreiser creates a mosaic of the experience of its two central characters in a specific time and place. Without such a range of detail, *Sister Carrie* would be simply another sentimental tale. Details are "things," and in Dreiser's brand of materialism, "things" determine the fortunes of men and women. It is through details that the reader recognizes the ironic rise and fall of Dreiser's characters.

The central theme of *Sister Carrie* is the effect of the misguided and misdirected American dream of success. The novel traces the separate but nonetheless individual stories of its characters in their efforts to realize the fabulous American dream. Carrie, seeking happiness and rising to stardom, reaches the verge of discovering personal fulfillment is an illusory dream. Money, clothes, and success fail to provide the happiness that they promise, but the darkest part of Carrie's tragedy is that she fails to understand this completely. Hurstwood, once having fallen from the "walled city" of the wealthy and influential, resigns himself too readily to failure and defeat. He also fails to recognize the shortcomings of a society whose values are based upon material things. Neither Carrie nor Hurstwood ever denies the values of the society that makes money its god. Charles Drouet, the "drummer," although he is relegated to the background midway through the novel, represents another important aspect of Dreiser's portrait. Drouet unconsciously assumes all the values of his day without a trace of rebellion. Thus, the figure of Drouet completes the picture by adding the tragedy of ignorance to Hurstwood's tragedy of failure and Carrie's tragedy of success.

In *Sister Carrie* Dreiser takes his central characters from the three classes of American economic life. He shows how they are harmed and corrupted by the fraudulent claims of the spurious American dream. The blame falls on the society that compels its individuals to become hideous and grotesque parodies of themselves.

## SYNOPSIS

In August, 1889, Caroline Meeber boards the train at her family home in Columbia City and travels to Chicago. Filled with fears, tears, and regrets, she is nonetheless determined to make her way in the big city.

On the long train ride she meets a handsome young traveling salesman named Charles Drouet. Shy at first, she is warmed and made confident by Drouet's easy manner and flashy clothes. He seems to her the epitome of wealth and influence. When the train arrives in Chicago, she and Drouet make plans to meet again the following week so that he can show her the sights of the city.

Carrie is met at the station by her sister Minnie Hanson. The two girls travel to the flat where Minnie lives with her husband Sven and their baby. The couple plan to have Carrie live with them while she works in the city. It is thought that Carrie will pay for her room and board in order to help the Hansons reduce expenses.

Carrie is thrilled by the prospect of finding work in Chicago. She imagines herself part of the great swirl of activity in the city. Her hopes are somewhat dampened when she finally obtains a job in a shoe factory at four and a half dollars a week.

Carrie realizes that she must abandon some of her more ambitious and fantastic plans. The Hansons disapprove of her wish to go to the theater. Minnie points out to Carrie that after paying four dollars for room and board, she will hardly have enough money left for carfare. Because the flat is so small, Carrie is unable to invite Drouet to visit.

As the cold winter sets in, Carrie finds that it is impossible to keep up the hard work at the factory. Finally, the combination of long hours, hard work, and inadequate clothing causes Carrie to become ill and she loses her job. The Hansons talk of sending her back to Columbia City, but she is determined to remain in Chicago.

One day as she wanders about downtown looking for a new job, she meets Drouet on the street. He buys her a splendid meal and "lends" her twenty dollars to buy decent clothes. Eventually he persuades Carrie to leave the Hansons and take a room of her own, offering to support her until she is settled. Soon Carrie and Drouet are living together in a cozy apartment. As time passes, Carrie perceives that Drouet is not nearly such an ideal figure as she had first imagined. He is egotistical and insensitive, but he is also kind and generous, and so she accepts her lot graciously. Drouet takes it upon himself to "educate" the untutored girl in the ways of society, teaching her to dress and behave according to fashion.

One evening the young couple are visited by George Hurstwood, a friend of Drouet's, the manager of a "way up, truly swell saloon." He is mature and attractive; he finds Carrie naive and pretty. The two are struck by an instantaneous fascination for each other and meet together frequently whenever the salesman is out of town.

Without Carrie's knowledge, Drouet enlists her talents as an actress in an amateur performance. To the surprise of Carrie, as well as her two admirers, the girl is a brilliant success. The next day Hurstwood confesses his love to Carrie and she responds favorably.

Eventually Drouet discovers that Carrie and Hurstwood have been seeing a great deal of each other and he moves out of the flat in order to frighten her. Hurstwood's wife, meanwhile, a shrewd and selfish woman, accuses Hurstwood of having an affair and initiates a divorce action against him.

One night when he stays late in his office to finish some paperwork, Hurstwood discovers that the safe has been left unlocked with over ten thousand dollars in it. While he is debating with himself whether to take the money, the door of the safe slams shut as he holds the entire amount in his hands. He is frightened and decides to flee. He rushes to Carrie's flat, tells her that Drouet has been injured and wishes to see her and whisks her away with him on a train to Canada.

Carrie is repelled by Hurstwood now, for she has learned from Drouet that he is married. Hurstwood argues that he has left his wife in order to be with Carrie. She believes him and agrees to remain with him if he will marry her.

In Canada, Hurstwood is tracked down by a private detective and returns most of the stolen money on the promise that his employers will not prosecute. The couple are married in a hasty ceremony, although the marriage is not valid.

The couple continue on to New York, where they find a comfortable apartment. Hurstwood is forced to invest the little money he has retained in a second-rate saloon. He and Carrie settle down to a routine existence in New York, never going out or meeting anyone.

Carrie strikes up a friendship with her neighbor, Mrs. Vance, a young lady of fine manners and expensive taste. Through the influence of Mrs. Vance and her cousin Bob Ames, Carrie begins to feel dissatisfied with being an ordinary housewife.

Hurstwood's business venture terminates and he finds himself unable to find employment. After a while he gives up searching and simply settles back to watch his meager savings dwindle. He loses his pride and dignity. He hardly ever leaves the house.

Conditions become so difficult that Carrie decides to find work. She eventually finds a part as a chorus girl in a Broadway "opera." Her fortunes rise steadily after that. Carrie decides to leave Hurstwood on his own, for he has become a deadweight to her.

In a few years Carrie gains fame and fortune as a stage comedienne. Hurstwood continues to decline until he becomes a Bowery tramp and finally commits suicide.

At the time of Hurstwood's suicide, Carrie has gained all that she had originally hoped for: wealth, finery, and prestige. Nevertheless she remains unsatisfied, always pondering the vagaries of fortune that make her desire something new and indefinable. It is clear that she will never gain the happiness she dreams of.

## LIST OF CHARACTERS

### Caroline (Carrie) Meeber

A naive young girl who goes to Chicago to seek her fortune and succumbs to the "cosmopolitan standard of virtue."

### Charles Drouet

A "drummer," or traveling salesman, who rescues Carrie from starvation and makes her his mistress.

### Minnie Hanson

Carrie's married elder sister, with whom she stays when she first arrives in Chicago.

### Sven Hanson

Minnie's husband, severe and practical.

### George Hurstwood

A friend of Drouet's who steals a great deal of money from his employers and virtually kidnaps Carrie. Once a pillar of society, he is later struck low by fortune.

### Julia Hurstwood

George Hurstwood's wife is a jealous, self-centered woman who is largely responsible for his ruin.

### Jessica Hurstwood

The Hurstwoods' snobbish, supercilious daughter is sixteen years old as the novel begins.

### George Hurstwood, Jr.

The Hurstwoods' son is nineteen at the beginning of the story. He is independent and self-important.

### Mrs. Frank Hale

An attractive thirty-five-year-old woman who has an apartment in the 29 Ogden Place building where Carrie lives with Drouet. Mrs. Hale stimulates Carrie's craving for wealth and elegance. Her husband is manager of the Standard theater.

### Harry Quincel

Member of the Custer Lodge of the Elks who supervises the amateur performance of Augustin Daly's *Under the Gaslight*.

### Mr. Millice

An imperious young man who directs the amateur production of *Under the Gaslight* at Avery Hall.

### Mrs. Morgan

A young woman who plays the part of Pearl in *Under the Gaslight*.

### Mr. Bamberger

Member of the original cast of *Under the Gaslight*. He is replaced in the part of Ray by Patton, a "loafing professional."

### Mr. Kenny

A Chicago stockbroker whom Hurstwood encounters in Montreal.

### Shaughnessy

Hurstwood's partner in the Warren Street bar in New York.

### Mrs. Vance

A young woman who sets Carrie's standards of taste in New York.

### Bob Ames

Cousin to Mrs. Vance; a studious young man whose serious view of life gives Carrie cause to question her own values.

### Mr. Cargill

Chicago stable-owner who meets Hurstwood by chance in New York.

### Lola Osborne

A young actress; Carrie's roommate and confidante.

## SUMMARIES AND COMMENTARIES

### CHAPTER 1

#### Summary

Caroline Meeber, an eighteen-year-old innocent, boards the train for her first trip to Chicago from her small home town in Wisconsin. Carrying all her worldly belongings, an imitation alligator satchel, a yellow purse, and four dollars in cash, she looks forward to Chicago with mixed timidity and hope, ignorance and youthful expectancy. As the train rushes out of town, all the bonds which tie her to childhood are irrevocably broken. Carrie is ignorant of the traps and disasters that lie in wait for her in the big city. It is certain that without someone to guide and counsel her she will fall prey to the cosmopolitan morality.

Aboard the train her prettiness and naivete attract the attention of a bold and dapper traveling salesman named Charles

Drouet. Although her maidenly reserve and sense of propriety forestall immediate familiarity with Drouet, she is gradually won over by the drummer's slangy charm. Because of the seeming shabbiness of her dress and her worn shoes, Carrie feels reticent and socially inferior to Drouet in his dashing attire. Soon, however, she becomes fascinated with Drouet's elegant appearance. In the lengthy conversation which ensues, Drouet flatters Carrie and finally obtains her Chicago address, making a tentative date to meet her again the following week.

As the train approaches the great city, Carrie sees the many telegraph poles set out in the still undeveloped prairie and solitary houses, "lone outposts of the approaching army of homes." Carrie is nearly transfixed by the sight of the city as they enter. When the train stops, she experiences a moment of terror and feels choked for breath so far away from Columbia City, her old home.

Once they are off the train, Drouet gallantly waits in the background for Carrie's sister Minnie to find her, and when she does, he departs with a smile that only Carrie sees. When Drouet disappears Carrie feels his absence greatly; she is "a lone figure in a tossing, thoughtless sea."

*Commentary*

In any novel, and particularly in *Sister Carrie*, the first chapter is extremely important. In it the author introduces his theme and plot through foreshadowing, careful arrangement of details, and introductory characterization. He begins the careful work of describing the setting. He introduces himself as the narrator of the story. Dreiser's attention to details is everywhere evident, from the description of Drouet's attire to the depiction of the outskirts of Chicago. Dreiser begins his story in such a way that Carrie herself is as unfamiliar with each situation as the reader is. Next to nothing is told of her life before leaving Columbia City, except for a few details that reveal how pedestrian it must have been.

By shifting between exposition and dramatic techniques, Dreiser succeeds in providing the reader with full information about Carrie without sacrificing any of the immediacy of her new venture. By carefully describing Carrie externally and internally, he manages to make the reader sympathetic as well as intimate with her. Thus, in a single paragraph it is revealed that Carrie "was possessed of a mind rudimentary in its power of observation and analysis" and also that she "could scarcely toss her head gracefully."

In dramatizing much of the first meeting of Carrie and Drouet, that is, by presenting it largely in dialog, Dreiser permits the Carrie he has already described to show herself in action. In addition to expository and dramatic techniques, part of Dreiser's method consists in making direct addresses to the reader, thus providing a thematic account of the action. By interpreting explicitly some of the story, Dreiser prepares the reader for interpreting other parts for himself. "When a girl leaves her home at eighteen, she does one of two things. Either she falls into saving hands and becomes better, or she rapidly assumes the cosmopolitan standard of virtue and becomes worse." When Carrie therefore finally accepts Drouet's bold overtures, the reader realizes that she is rapidly assuming the "cosmopolitan standard" and that her virtue is likely to suffer.

Carrie's keen interest in attractive clothing and the deficiency of her own clothing is an integral part of the future outcome of the novel. Much of Carrie's story is presented in terms of the clothing she acquires.

Foreshadowing occurs throughout the chapter; the title of the chapter itself—"The Magnet Attracting: A Waif Amid Forces"—is significant. The forceful Drouet flatters the impressionable Carrie by saying that she resembles a popular actress of the day. In a few short years Carrie will actually become a famous stage personality. Finally, the last image of Carrie adrift in the sea, bobbing endlessly, is one that will reappear in various forms throughout the novel.

## CHAPTERS 2-4

*Summary*

Minnie takes her sister Carrie to the flat where she lives with her husband and baby. The flat is small and poorly furnished. Sven Hanson, Minnie's husband, works long hours in the stockyards while Minnie remains at home occupied with the steady toil of caring for the child and keeping house. The whole workaday atmosphere of the flat contrasts with the bustle of activity of the city itself and with Carrie's expectations.

Carrie writes to Drouet that she cannot see him again because the flat is much too small for visitors. Then she sits quietly in a rocking chair before going to bed. In the morning she takes a trip to the manufacturing area of the city, where she can think only of people counting money, dressing magnificently, and riding in carriages. The enormous cluster of warehouses and factories strikes her with awe, and she shrinks away from the notion of asking any of these mighty men for a chance to earn a day's pay.

Finally, she meekly asks for employment at several places but is turned away. Carrie finds herself adrift in the afternoon rush of the city, but finally a job offer at four and a half dollars per week raises her spirits. The foreman who hires Carrie looks her over if she were a package, for this is a world where individuals are of no real importance. Once again, she looks forward to the pleasure and amusement of the city and the company of Drouet.

For the next two days Carrie speculates concerning the amusements and privileges that will fall her way. Minnie wonders if her sister will make enough money to pay for carfare after paying her four dollars room and board. Carrie arouses a shade of disapproval when she suggests that Minnie and Sven go with her to the theater, where a popular melodrama is playing. Minnie and Sven are rather disappointed with Carrie's strong craving for pleasure, the "one stay of her nature." Unless Carrie submits to a solemn round of industry and realizes the necessity of hard and steady work, her presence will afford the Hansons no economic advantages.

Carrie does not go to the theater. Friday night is spent loitering on the front stairs of the apartment building. On Saturday Carrie walks through a more fashionable part of the city and wonders whether Drouet will call on Monday after all. Arising at six o'clock on Monday morning, Carrie eats her breakfast in silence, wondering about her new job. She has a vague feeling that she will come in contact with the "great owners" and that she will be performing her work in a place where well-dressed men will look upon her with interest. Her first day of work is a nightmare. She is a link in a chain; she must at once keep up with the average speed of the assembly line or all those beyond her station will be delayed.

Carrie works incessantly for a time, finding relief for her fears in the dull, mechanical operation of the machinery. As the morning wears on slowly, the room becomes hotter and the work becomes even more tedious. She sits on a backless stool working without fresh air or water. When she stands up to work, cramps develop in her neck and shoulders.

Besides the tedious nature of the work, there is the unending and inane chatter of the other girls and the brazen advances of the young men for her to contend with. The work becomes nearly unbearable; Carrie's body is wracked with aches and pains; her eyes are strained. Then the dull bell clangs for lunch.

Her co-workers fill her with such disgust with their catty badinage and useless conversation that Carrie is glad when the half-hour lunch period is over and the work begins again. Wondering if the dull routine will ever stop, she continues the monotonous operation until six o'clock. As she walks home Carrie thinks that she deserves something more than a lifetime of such work and her spirit protests.

## Commentary

The main point of these three chapters is to suggest Carrie's inability to understand either the mechanical lives of the Hansons or the superhuman activity of the rapidly growing city. Neither the Hanson household nor the city takes time to slacken the daily pace to admit her gradually. It is revealed that the Hansons are counting upon Carrie to help them reduce household expenses. The city offers no interesting employment to someone as inexperienced as Carrie.

In the department store Carrie realizes how far removed she is from its glamor and attraction. Although she desires for herself the frilly dresses, the jewelry and trinkets heaped upon the counters, she keenly feels how none of these are in the range of her purchase. "An outcast without employment," a mere job-seeker, even the shopgirls could see she was poor and in need of a paying job.

Nevertheless, observing the attire and manner of both the shopgirls and the patrons, Carrie sees how much the city holds in the way of wealth, fashion, and ease, and she longs for luxury with her whole heart. Then, filled with optimism, she begins to think of the city once more as a "great, pleasing metropolis," a place where she will live and be happy. Dreiser's belief that a person's financial condition determines the manner in which he perceives the world is evident throughout these chapters: in Carrie's materialistic response to the wealth of the city lies a great deal of the plot of the novel.

When Carrie begins to work, her naive expectations are quickly driven underground by the dull, hard routine of the assembly line. Not only does she suffer physically, but she is insulted and abused by the young men who work in the factory. The detailed description of the work which Carrie must perform and her revulsion to it contrast sharply with her vague and extravagant desires and speculations about the future. Instead of well-dressed and gracious owners Carrie finds a gruff foreman who seems a very ogre. Instead of finding exciting work that would be a challenge to her intellect and imagination, she finds herself chained to a machine in a room full of nearly mechanical people.

In his effort to leave a well-documented record of a time that has passed, Dreiser departs from the story line to describe how inferior working conditions were even when compared with those of twenty years later. Carrie and the others perform the same laborious task all day without benefit of a change in routine or a brief rest. The hours are long, the factory is without proper lighting or ventilation. No effort is made for the employees' comfort, in the belief that hard conditions are advantageous.

Nor does Dreiser overlook the symbolic import of the assembly line and the workhouse. Work in a factory is very similar to the grand scale of life as he saw it. Each individual becomes a cog in a wheel; each is a package of energy. The poor and weak are exploited by the strong and wealthy. Such conditions make dull animals of all they encompass. The weaker of the species must be sacrificed to the stronger; this is the ethos of cut-throat capitalism.

The poor working conditions, the uncouth boys, the long hours, and the tedium all serve to make Drouet stand out in Carrie's mind as the epitome of the good life. Carrie constantly compares her experiences with her memory of Drouet, who gains much by the contrast. Carrie is learning the hard lesson that drives its wedge between expectation and reality. Knowing as much as he does about Carrie's character and her strivings for pleasure, the reader wonders what will become of Carrie in the grotesque world she has fallen into. Carrie had hoped to visit the theater and wear fine clothes, but already she is trapped by economic conditions. Although her spirit rebels, she seems resigned to her fate.

## CHAPTER 5

### Summary

Because of the letter, Drouet does not visit Carrie on Monday evening. After dining in a rather exclusive restaurant, he stops in at Fitzgerald and Moy's saloon to have a drink with the manager, his friend George Hurstwood. After a brief discussion of business associates and acquaintances, Drouet leaves for the theater. Just as he is leaving, Drouet mentions the "little peach" he met on the train, but Hurstwood is unimpressed.

## Commentary

Most of this short chapter consists of Dreiser's commentary on the manner in which social status is achieved and maintained. Drouet dines frequently at Rector's because it is a resort for actors and professional men and thus it inflates his vanity and stirs his ambition. For the same reason he seeks the comforts of Fitzgerald and Moy's saloon, which Dreiser describes in his awkward style as a "truly swell saloon."

The introduction of Hurstwood, who some critics believe is the central character of the novel, shows him to be just under forty, vigorous, urbane, and distinguished by fine clothing and conservative good taste. Hurstwood is of that class of people who bow only to the luxuriously rich. He maintains a rigidly graduated scale of informality and friendship which covers all patrons of the "gorgeous saloon."

Dreiser embarks on a discussion of the institution of the men's saloon. Visitors there seek pleasure as well as the satisfaction of shining among their betters. In a society which equates wealth with individual worth, the worst such an institution would do is stir up the ambition of the materialist, such as Drouet, so that he too could conduct his life on a splendid basis. It is not the richness of the establishment which does this, however; it is the inner workings of the mind. This is the genuine masculine counterpart of the world of Carrie's dreams — fine clothes and manners, wealth, position, and enjoyment.

By implication Dreiser says that to a newcomer this saloon must seem a "strange and shiny thing." Then with a measure of irony he adds, "what a lamp-flower it must bloom; a strange, glittering night-flower, odor-yielding, insect-drawing,

26

insect-infested rose of pleasure." Thus by contrasting what such a place seems to its regular patrons with what it would seem to an outsider, Dreiser as narrator invites the reader to see the aimlessly wandering, dressy, greedy company as not terribly different from Carrie herself, only "luckier" and wealthier.

The thematic and structural import of the chapter lies in its final paragraph. Determined to show the inexplicable workings of fate, Dreiser provides justification for diverting the reader's attention away from Carrie so early in the novel. The story of Carrie will be the story of Drouet and Hurstwood as well: "Thus was Carrie's name bandied about in the most frivolous and gay of places, and that also when the little toiler was bemoaning her narrow lot, which was almost inseparable from the early stages of this, her unfolding fate."

## CHAPTERS 6-7

### Summary

That same evening Carrie returns home from her first day of work. To Minnie and Sven's anxious questioning, she answers that she does not like her job because it is too hard. Minnie feels sympathetic toward Carrie but hides her feelings because she knows how much Sven is counting on the extra money Carrie could contribute to the household.

After supper Carrie changes her clothes and stands on the steps of the apartment building, half expecting to see Drouet. The life on the street interests Carrie. She never ties of wondering where its streetcars are going or how the people on them entertain themselves. Her imagination constantly takes her to places of delight, full of handsome, well-dressed, and wealthy people enjoying themselves.

The daily work at the factory continues in its hard, dull routine. At the end of a week Carrie hands over four dollars to Minnie, keeping fifty cents for herself. Like a flower that is transplanted, Carrie has trouble adjusting to the climate. Winter sweeps over the city before Carrie can save enough money to buy warm clothes. She is taken ill and must rest in bed for three days. Hanson wants Carrie to return to her family before she becomes a burden.

After she recovers from her cold, Carrie searches four full days for a new position until, quite by accident, she meets Drouet. Surprised to see her, he buys her a sumptuous steak in an expensive restaurant. To Carrie, Drouet seems the very picture of substantial living. Well-dressed and outspoken, he impresses Carrie with his knowledge of faraway places and with his easy manners. Carrie nevertheless refuses to join him at the theater because she cannot stay out late, but she does agree to meet him the next day.

Drouet forces upon Carrie a "loan" of twenty dollars for her to buy herself new shoes and a jacket. Carrie feels "as though a great arm had slipped out before her to draw off trouble." In Drouet's presence Carrie does not even think that Minnie will wonder where the new clothes came from, but as soon as she leaves Drouet she begins to worry.

The narrator begins Chapter 7 with one of his frequent discussions on the meaning of money. What Carrie does not understand, a fault she has in common with almost all of humanity, is that money should be paid out as "honestly stored energy," not as a "usurped privilege." Carrie's definition of money would be simple and straightforward— "something everybody else has and I must get."

As she walks away from Drouet Carrie feels ashamed that she had been weak enough to take his money, but since her needs were so desperate, she is glad to have the power of privilege that "two soft, green, handsome ten-dollar bills" can bring. As usual, her visions of what she can purchase—a nice new jacket, a pair of button shoes, stockings, a skirt—far exceed the reality.

Carrie fully realizes that unlike the stranger who accosted her in the street some days before, Drouet is of good heart and intends no evil. There is nothing in his character to trigger her instinct to fly away from him. His overtures do not arouse her sense of self-preservation.

When she reaches home, Carrie's good feelings are somewhat dampened because she can imagine no way to explain her good fortune to Minnie. Ironically trapped, having money and not being able to spend it, Carrie resolves to return the money to Drouet the next day. The next morning she returns to the wholesale district and wanders about, trying only one place for work. Carrie enters a large department store, where she is torn between material desire and moral conscience. Indecision continues until it is time for her to meet Drouet. Drouet takes charge of things and causes Carrie to buy a new jacket, button shoes, and stockings, to which he adds a purse and gloves. Then he helps her find a furnished room where she can deposit the new finery and even move in herself if she desires.

In the evening Carrie returns to the flat for dinner with Minnie and Sven. After dinner she writes a note explaining that she is leaving them but she is not returning to Columbia City. She will remain in Chicago and look for work. She then announces that she will stand outside for the last time. Nearby Drouet is waiting for her; together the couple leave the neighborhood in a streetcar.

## Commentary

Carrie begins to realize that her ties with her sister and brother-in-law are merely economic. As a companion and confidante, Minnie is of no worth to Carrie. The struggle for survival in the big city has destroyed in her any of the soft qualities that bind sisters together. Carrie is not given to sentimental notions, however, and so the subversion of sisterly relations does not bother her. She would sooner realize her imaginary wealth and pleasure than find lasting human relationships.

By showing Carrie again and again moving through the same dull routine, day after day, Dreiser presents rather than describes the tedious nature of Carrie's life. It is obvious to the reader that Carrie's imagination will not allow her to continue on this treadmill very much longer. By dramatizing little incidents, such as her reaction to the passes made at her by the young men at work, Dreiser accomplishes far more than ordinary description could do. The continued repetition involves the reader in the mechanical round of activities. By sympathizing with Carrie, the reader is willing to overlook her minor indiscretions.

In the midst of these activities Dreiser makes an analogy between Carrie and a flower. Carrie is no part of this mechanical world; she is a growing organism which may blossom, but she requires richer soil and a better climate even to continue her natural growth. Abrupt transplantation is dangerous to the tender plant. The analogy becomes even more striking when one remembers that cruel winter is setting in, making it continually more difficult for plants to grow. Overall conditions, in fact—the urgent necessity for finding work, the nature of the work itself and situations in the factory, Carrie's lack of proper clothing or money to buy it, the attitudes of Minnie and Sven—combine to make Carrie physically ill.

Although a perceivable set of conditions causes Carrie to become ill and lose her job, it is fate or chance which causes Carrie and Drouet to meet once again on the downtown street. Dreiser frequently refers to Carrie as a "little solider of fortune"; although she is not herself aware of it, Carrie is a follower of the fate of human existence.

In Drouet's presence, Carrie feels thoroughly at ease and sees the world clearly. Through Drouet the world reveals more of its possibilities. She becomes something of an insider of the world of wealth, fashion, and pleasure. She cannot think of the complications his "loan" will create, but when he is gone she is once again cast into a sea of doubt and indecision.

X   The story of Carrie Meeber is at all times the story of a young and innocent girl who must suddenly find her way in an alien metropolis. Beyond that story is the tale of a young and naive America coming of age. In many respects Carrie is similar to Isabel Archer in Henry James' novel, *The Portrait of a Lady*. Carrie might easily be seen in retrospect as the backwoods, small-town American society emerging from innocence to the cosmopolitan standards of the end of the nineteenth century. By bringing to bear upon Carrie the economic and fateful determinism that so thoroughly pervaded the thought of his own day, Dreiser makes of her a symbolic figure who must sacrifice a certain amount of innocence in order to make progress of any kind. Thus Carrie's dream is the American Dream as well; it is a dream of rich finery, financial success, and power. Like America itself, Carrie must learn not only how to acquire her wealth and power, but must also learn the meaning and extent and correct use of these.

Drouet's character is one that requires careful analysis. He is a "nice, good-hearted man." There is nothing evil in Drouet, but he is an opportunist. Drouet is largely unreflective and unphilosophical. "In his good clothes and fine health, he was a merry, unthinking moth of the lamp." With only a sudden change in fortune for him, he, too, would become as helpless as Carrie.

Despite his continued success with women, Drouet is no man of the world. He would be as easily "hornswaggled" by a villain as an ordinary shopgirl might be duped by him. Unlike Carrie, Drouet shows no potential for growth and change. His ambition is directed toward material success and display and affable company. He does not share Carrie's inner dissatisfaction with the world as it is. He lacks the imagination necessary to be prone to brooding and emotional decisions.

On the very first page of the novel Dreiser writes that when a young girl leaves home, she does one of two things. "Either she falls into saving hands and becomes better, or she rapidly assumes the cosmopolitan standard of virtue and becomes worse. Of an intermediate balance, under the circumstances, there is no possibility." The major portion of *Sister Carrie* is devoted to exploring the implications of that statement. Here in this chapter is found a variation on that theme. Although Drouet does put forth a hand to save Carrie, his gesture requires that she change her standards of virtue. The rapid change effected in Carrie's nature is given specific form in the department store. Deciding the night before to return Drouet's money intact, she avoids spending it, not because of her staunch virtue, but because of indecision. Carrie is apt to put off decisions until it becomes too late for her to do anything. Very often she is the bark that is swept along on the enormous sea with the tide. By avoiding decisions, Carrie entrusts herself to fate.

The question of Dreiser's writing style deserves special attention (see notes on Dreiser's Style), but, awkward as it is, it is still the product of conscious craft. In the following passage, Dreiser makes masterful use of rhythm, punctuation, strategic placing of adjectives, inflation, and deflation. The movement of the passage imitates the movement of Carrie's mind: "Now she would have a nice new jacket! Now she would buy a nice pair of pretty button shoes. She would get stockings, too, and a skirt, and, and—until already, as in the matter of her prospective salary, she had got beyond, in her desires, twice the purchasing power of her bills." This is style at its best.

# CHAPTERS 8-10

*Summary*

Very early the next morning Minnie awakes to find Carrie's note. Minnie is severely upset because she knows what ill fortune might befall a young girl alone in the city. Hanson is not the least upset by Carrie's departure; he is probably glad to be rid of her.

Already Carrie's life has changed significantly, for even while the Hansons are discussing her departure, she is sound asleep in a furnished room of her own in another part of the city. When Drouet calls to take her out to breakfast, she tells him that she is anxious to begin looking for work again. Drouet sweeps away her worrying by telling her not to hurry, to take her time seeing the city and getting "fixed up." The conversation turns to Carrie's new clothes and Drouet's promise to buy her more. With that, her misgivings about leaving the Hansons and her anxiety over what Drouet intends to do with her are cast aside.

The couple spend their days together shopping and sight-seeing. Carrie gradually begins to realize how pretty she is and begins to feel the thrill of being an attractive well-dressed woman with a gallant escort. In the evenings they visit the theater and dine in the more fashionable restaurants of the city.

One evening as Carrie and Drouet are walking to the theater while the rest of the world is hurrying home from work, a pair of eyes meets Carrie's in recognition. The eyes are those of one of the factory girls with whom Carrie used to work: she is poorly dressed in shabby garments. As the two exchange glances, Carrie feels "as if some great tide had rolled between them. The old dress and the old machine came back." Carrie is so startled that she bumps into a pedestrian.

Stopping for an after-theater snack, Carrie is not troubled by the lateness of the hour or any household law which will drag her home. The combined influence of the many occurrences of the day makes Carrie relaxed and carefree, once again a victim of the city's hypnotic powers.

Drouet walks Carrie to the house where she is staying and, although it is only suggested by Dreiser, it seems safe to assume that he asks Carrie to live with him. While Carrie and Drouet stand on the doorstep, sister Minnie dreams a succession of nightmares. In her several dreams Minnie and Carrie stand together at the brink of a dark precipice and then Carrie slips away and falls out of sight.

About a week later Drouet strolls into Fitzgerald and Moy's to invite his friend Hurstwood to spend an evening with him and Carrie. Hurstwood accepts warmly.

He is always glad to get away from his family and home life, for there are no bonds of understanding. Although the house is fashionably and opulently appointed, it lacks warmth. His children are irresponsible and snobbish; his wife is a social climber and a bit of a shrew.

The Hurstwood household, the narrator concludes, "ran along by force of habit, by force of conventional opinion. With the lapse of time it must necessarily become dryer and dryer— must eventually be tinder, easily lighted and destroyed."

Now that Carrie and Drouet have set up housekeeping, Drouet is pleased by his conquest; Carrie is at times full of somber misgivings. Drouet has rented a small furnished apartment in Ogden Place, facing Union Park. Through Carrie's "industry and natural love of order," the place is made very pleasing.

Carrie's difficulties, more basic in the recent past, have now become mental ones, "and altogether so turned about in all of her earthly relationships that she might well have been a new and different individual." In the mirror she sees a pretty face, but when she looks within herself she sees an image composed of her own judgments and those of society that makes her experience a certain moral queasiness. Carrie wavers between these two reflections, wondering which one to embrace. Her conscience, "only an average little conscience," is shaped by the world, her own past life, habit, and convention, all welded together in a confused way. Her conscience bothers her because she failed to live with moral correctness even before she tried. Carrie is in a "winter" mood, full of silent brooding. Nevertheless the secret voice of her conscience grows more and more feeble.

Drouet is together with Carrie most of the time, except for sporadic, short business trips. Drouet continually procrastinates about marriage to Carrie, telling her there is a business deal he must close before he can give himself over to thoughts of legal marriage. Carrie seeks marriage, for that would salve her conscience and justify her actions of late. Carrie herself knows that she feels no special love for Drouet, but she thinks that marriage would be insurance against losing his affection and generosity.

Hurstwood arrives and deports himself with a grace and polish that the young Drouet lacks. Accustomed to pleasing men in his work, Hurstwood is even more tactful and attentive to pretty women in his desire to please them and be of service. His conservative but rich apparel further contrasts him to Drouet. Carrie compares little details, such as the dull shine of Hurstwood's black calf shoes with Drouet's shiny patent leather shoes, and she favors the soft rich leather.

The three play euchre, a card game popular at the time. Hurstwood behaves so deferentially and warmly that even Drouet feels closer to him than ever before. In Carrie's presence Hurstwood replaces his everyday "shifty, clever gleam" of the eyes with geniality and kindness and innocence.

Hurstwood contrives the game so that Carrie wins all the dimes that they have been playing for. He invites them to go to the theater with him before Drouet's impending trip. Hurstwood reveals his "magnanimity" by offering to visit Carrie when Drouet is out of town and Carrie and Drouet remark how kind he is. After a snack and a bottle of wine, Hurstwood leaves the young couple nearly dazed by his charm.

### Commentary

One aspect of Dreiser's "naturalistic" method which a good many critics find fault with is his frequent and lengthy editorial intrusions. It is characteristic of Dreiser's method to present a repetitive discussion of fate or morality and then drive home the point by showing a character undergoing nearly the same process of thought. It is up to the individual reader to discover for himself whether this method is entirely successful. Chapter 9 opens with a short essay on the relationship of morality and evolution. Mankind in his present state of civilization is scarcely a beast in that he is no longer wholly guided by instinct; neither is he completely human, because he is not yet wholly guided by reason. Mankind must constantly waver between instinctual harmony with nature or rational harmony with his own free will.

Carrie finds herself in such a position. Her instincts and desires have driven her to Drouet, but her reason and understanding cause her to have misgivings about it. In the statement, "She was as yet more drawn than she drew," the future of Carrie's self-control is suggested. Worldly experience will teach her to align her instincts with her reason.

In the episode where Carrie meets one of the girls with whom she used to work she sees what a great tide had rolled between the nearly animal existence of the past and her present situations. Her "vain imaginings" reveal to her what it is to be "wholly human," to have power and position and to conduct herself as her reason or will would permit. To Carrie as well as to Dreiser, the presence of wealth and fine clothing indicates a wide freedom of choice. Thus, those "magnificent people" are more closely aligned with free will.

The two antithetical portions of Carrie's mind, her conscience and her desire, make another appearance in Chapter 10. There, standing before the mirror, she sees that her face reveals a more attractive girl than she was before but that her mind, "a mirror prepared of her own and the world's opinions," reveals a "worse" creature than she had been before. She wavers between these two images, uncertain of which one to believe.

The "inner" mirror, the reservoir of social and acquired moral opinion, must be watched closely by the reader. *Sister Carrie* is a study in depth of character; what happens inside Carrie's mind is actually far more important than her outward fortune or trials and tribulation.

Dream symbolism provides a method of revealing what the world outside thinks of Carrie's behavior. Minnie, Carrie's sister, functions in the novel as a *choric* figure. In her dream is revealed what the standard judgment of Carrie's actions would be. Carrie is leaving the world of her sister to go to a dark and dangerous world below the surface of the ground. The swirling waters or unplumbed darkness of that world without a rigid morality seem certain to destroy the naive girl. It is no more necessary to accept Minnie's dream as absolute truth, however, than it is to accept Carrie's estimate of her sister Minnie as absolute and unbiased truth. Each girl unconsciously sees the other as a projection of herself, and thus interprets the life of the other as it would seem to herself. In the structure of the novel Carrie and Minnie, as well as Drouet and Hurstwood, are paired for comparison and contrast.

The irony of Carrie's belief that wealthy people have an unlimited freedom of choice is made apparent by the description of Hurstwood's family life. Hurstwood is practically a stranger in his own home, but his position is so inextricably related to his home life that he can make no changes: "He could not complicate his home life, because it might affect his relations with his employers. They wanted no scandals. A man, to hold his position, must have a dignified manner." It is ironic also that it is Carrie herself who will eventually cause Hurstwood to "complicate" his condition. Still another irony appears in these chapters; this takes the form of ironic foreshadowing. To Drouet's remark, after Hurstwood ends his visit, that he is a "nice man" and a "good friend," Carrie responds with unconscious irony, "He seems to be."

Very often readers of Dreiser take his seeming simplicity of technique too lightly, even though it should be apparent that he possesses a talent for making symbolic use of ordinary details. Thus, for example, in the card game played at the first meeting of Carrie and Hurstwood, Dreiser provides a microcosm, or miniature model, of the characters, forces, and movement of the novel. In this game of chance and skill Hurstwood manipulates his hand so that Carrie can win all the money while Drouet remains ignorant of what is happening. "Don't you moralize," Hurstwood says to Carrie, "until you see what becomes of the money."

*Summary*

Carrie continues to grow more graceful and charming as the days pass. Drouet seeks to help along her change by making tactless and stupidly cruel comparisons with other women; he has no awareness of Carrie's extreme sensitivity. One evening as she sits alone listening to a piano being played in the next apartment she is moved to tears by the combination of its wistful sadness and her own mood. She is crying when Drouet arrives; he makes the absurd suggestion that they waltz to the music. "It was his first great mistake."

Returning from a business trip one evening, Drouet meets an old female acquaintance and invites her to dinner. To the chagrin of Drouet, Hurstwood enters the same restaurant and sees the two together. Drouet feels embarrassed and guilty, thinking correctly that Hurstwood will interpret this as a sign that Drouet is already growing tired of Carrie.

A few days later the couple receives an invitation from Hurstwood to join him at the theater. Carrie is concerned that Drouet might notice her readiness to break an engagement for Hurstwood that she was reluctant to break for him. His egotism is so strong, however, that the detail escapes his notice. Carrie recognizes not only that Hurstwood is the superior man, but also that he looks upon her with more than companionable affection. Drouet is losing Carrie's heart as quickly as Hurstwood gains it, but he is too sure of himself ever to suspect this.

In the meantime, Mrs. Hurstwood suspects her husband's tendencies, although she is not yet aware of his "moral defection." It is her nature to wait and brood upon revenge. Because much of his property is in her name Hurstwood behaves very carefully, since he could not be sure what she might do if she became dissatisfied. Realizing that all love between them has been lost over the years, Hurstwood is inclined to turn his back on the relationship, but Mrs. Hurstwood expects complete adherence to the forms of marriage, even though the spirit has waned. Nevertheless, Hurstwood begins to excuse himself more and more from family and social matters.

His interest in "Drouet's little shopgirl" grows in proportion to his marital discontent. As for Carrie herself, she begins to acquire a sense of taste and wealth which guides her desire. Her neighbor, Mrs. Hale, with whom she walks and rides frequently, awakens the "siren voice of the unrestful" whispering in Carrie's ear. Sadly, Carrie longs for the power of affluence, which she is certain dispels all care and bestows every felicity.

One afternoon after a drive with Mrs. Hale, Carrie sits at home in her rocking chair by the window, feeling lonely and forsaken. Although she has seen little of Hurstwood through the long winter, she has kept him in mind by the strong impression their few meetings together had made on her. The manager arrives at that moment, and his presence and graceful manner and warmth cause Carrie to brighten until "all her best side is exhibited." Hurstwood's glances and light touches of the hand are as effective upon Carrie as the spoken words of a lover. They require no immediate decision or answer, only a warm response. Eventually, Hurstwood forces Carrie to admit that she is unhappy and .dissatisfied with her life as it is. She becomes distressed by her own frankness and when Hurstwood departs, troubled and ashamed, she looks into the mirror, saying aloud, "I'm getting terrible...I don't seem to do anything right."

Hurstwood feels that a liaison with Carrie would provide him with a new opportunity for real life. Carrie's youth, naivete, and vitality seem to compensate for all the deceit experience has led him to find in women. He wants to win Carrie and sincerely believes that "her fate mingled with his" would be far "better than if it were united with Drouet's."

Carrie compares the two men in her mind and sees that Drouet is the type who carries the "doom of all enduring relationships in his own lightsome manner and unstable fancy." He is too youthful to grieve long over a departed lover. She does realize, however, that Hurstwood has not yet formulated any plans except to accelerate the progress of their affection for each other.

Two days after their previous meeting, Hurstwood returns once again and he and Carrie go for a walk. Because he feels that he might be seen by someone who should not see him, Hurstwood suggests that they take a drive on the Boulevard, a country road where houses are just beginning to appear.

Hurstwood turns on his full passionate charm, confessing to Carrie that he loves her. This produces no visible effect, so he turns next to an appeal to her pity. Carrie can form no words or even thoughts; but she sees that Hurstwood's complaint of having no one to sympathize with him or show more than indifference is her complaint as well.

"Tell me that you love me," says Hurstwood. "Own to it." Carrie makes no answer but simply responds to Hurstwood's kiss. He asks then if she is now his "own girl." In response, she lays her head upon his shoulder.

### Commentary

Chapters 11, 12, and 13 might well be subtitled "Hurstwood's Courtship of Carrie." The courtship is simply one more variation on the theme of forbidden love, and its development is self-explanatory. Nevertheless, Dreiser's employment of imagery, symbol, and setting warrants some attention. The wresting away of Carrie from Drouet is presented with the imagery of battle and games. After the theater, Drouet is not aware "that a battle had been fought and his defenses weakened. He was like the Emperor of China, who sat glorying in himself, unaware that his fairest provinces were being wrested from him." On the way home, Drouet foolishly leaves Carrie to go to the forward platform of the streetcar to smoke, "and left the game as it stood." (For the relevance of games, see Commentary on Chapter 10.)

Another important source of imagery throughout the novel is the sea. When Hurstwood asks Carrie (in Chapter 12) if she is unhappy, she is described as "getting into deep water" and "letting her few supports float away from her." The prairie outside the city, a "flat, open scene," resembles the sea when Hurstwood confesses his love to Carrie. Throughout the novel Carrie experiences "floods" of emotion and frequently "drifts" off into thought. Hurstwood tells Carrie that before he met her, he was wont to "drift" about. Many times Carrie is shown rocking endlessly in a chair as if she were "a lone figure in a tossing, thoughtless sea."

The rocking chair itself is a symbol of Carrie's continued frustration and her inability to make a choice, wavering instead from one possibility to the other. Just before the first of Hurstwood's two visits which occur in these chapters Carrie sits rocking in her chair. Dreiser takes the opportunity to foreshadow the future outcome of her desire: "She hummed and hummed as the moments went by...and was therein as happy though she did not perceive it, as she ever would be."

Another important symbol is the mirror in which Carrie attempts to see inside herself to discover the truth or to reflect upon some problem. Like the rocking chair, the mirror represents the two poles of Carrie's thought, for it is also used by her simply to admire her appearance in new clothes. Both the rocking chair and the mirror fuse the desire for material satisfaction with the realization that Carrie is never happy if she continually desires something new. Naturally, Carrie is never conscious of the symbolic import of these articles, but certainly the author is, and so, it is hoped, is the reader.

The events of these particular chapters occur in the spring, traditionally a time of the emergence or reawakening of love. Hurstwood's attraction to Carrie seems "a flowering out of feelings which had been withering in dry and almost barren soil for many years." In a touch of humor rarely found in Dreiser, Hurstwood is overheard telling his wife that he saw the play "Rip Van Winkle" with Carrie and Drouet. In Carrie's presence Hurstwood feels as fresh as "one who is taken out of the flash of summer to the first cool breath of spring." References to the season abound throughout these chapters and provide a steady counterpoint to the frequent mention of winter in the first ten chapters. Carrie's affair with Drouet had been in the winter, but her new love occurs in the spring. On the prairie, as Hurstwood slips his arm about Carrie, "A breath of soft spring wind went bounding over the road, rolling some brown twigs of the previous autumn before it."

Attention has been called earlier to the method in which Drouet occasionally interrupts the narrative to present an idea or comment or theory, then eventually causes a character or situation to repeat the theme of the discussion in a different light. A fine example of this technique appears in Chapters 12 and 13. Dreiser interrupts a conversation between Carrie and Hurstwood to offer the following comment: "People in general attach too much importance to words. They are under the illusion that talking effects great results. As a matter of fact, words are, as a rule, the shallowest portion of all the argument. They but dimly represent the great surging feelings and desires which lie behind. When the distraction of the tongue is removed, the heart listens."

In Hurstwood and Carrie there appear, respectively, one who attaches "too much importance to words" and one whose "heart listens." Thus at the close of Chapter 13 Hurstwood repeatedly tries to spill out his thoughts and feelings in words and tries to require the same of Carrie. Carrie, sensitive soul that she is, can only respond with looks and gestures. Throughout the progress of their attachment, Carrie has been aware of the meaning of Hurstwood's glances and gestures, but he seems to require that she spell out her emotions in careful words and well-formed phrases.

## CHAPTERS 14-15

### Summary

Even as her neighbor Mrs. Hale is spreading gossip about the rooming house, Carrie reflects on her situation with Drouet and begins to see hope of a way out, mistakenly perceiving in Hurstwood an advance toward honor and self-respect.

Hurstwood, however, thinks only of "pleasure without responsibility." He wishes to do nothing that would "complicate his life." During their next meeting Hurstwood realizes that Carrie takes their love "on a much higher basis" than he believed. She holds him off, granting only "tokens of affection." Hurstwood sees that Carrie will be no easy conquest and so resolves to control his ardor.

Hurstwood pretends to believe that Carrie is actually married to Drouet, and hopes that Drouet will not tell Carrie that he has a wife and family. When Drouet returns home from his business trip, Carrie once again poses the question of marriage. Of course Drouet does not plan to marry her, even in the distant future. Carrie therefore feels justified in her affair with Hurstwood, believing that it will lead to the secure and honorable state of matrimony.

Drouet and Carrie accept an invitation from Hurstwood to attend the theater. A secret letter to Carrie from Hurstwood asks her to meet him in the afternoon before the performance. At that time the lovers agree not to show any interest in each other when Drouet is present.

That evening, Hurstwood is particularly attentive to his old friend Drouet and strives to avoid "that subtle ridicule which a lover in favor may so secretly practice before the mistress of his heart." It is difficult, because in the play *The Covenant,* a young wife listens willingly to her seductive lover while her husband is away. "Served him right," remarks Drouet, speaking of the husband, "I haven't any pity for a man who would be such a chump as that." Hurstwood answers gently that "you can never tell"; perhaps the man thought he was right.

Emerging from the theater Hurstwood is approached by a panhandler but, blinded by the presence of Carrie, he does not even see the fellow. The good-natured Drouet quickly responds to the man's plight "with an upwelling feeling of pity in his heart." The occurrence is scarcely noticed by the lovers.

At home, the details of Hurstwood's marriage show that it is going into a crisis. He is continually more put off by his wife's self-centered demands and his children's shallow behavior. Hurstwood begins writing daily letters to Carrie from his office. Each new sentence allows him to feel the subtleties that he tries to express. He loves Carrie for her youth, beauty, and her good nature. She is sympathetic and kind to him and full of pity for all who suffer. All these qualities make Carrie a "waxen lily" in Hurstwood's eyes. He begins to feel youthful himself.

The lovers meet in the park to discuss the future. Carrie says that she is willing to leave Drouet anytime if Hurstwood consents to marry her. Her refusal merely to become his mistress causes Hurstwood to be even more in love with her. To test her affection for him, Hurstwood asks with unconscious irony if she would leave Chicago with him without notice. Of course she will, if he will marry her, is the reply. Hurstwood did not mean the question to be taken so seriously. He replies jokingly, "I'll come and get you one of these evenings," and then laughs.

### Commentary

It is necessary to consider Carrie's motives in allowing herself to forsake Drouet for Hurstwood. She recognizes that Drouet is not interested in building any kind of sincere relationship. His interest in Carrie is kindled by his own desires for pleasure and his egotistical good nature. He has chosen to make of Carrie a kind of Pygmalion's Galatea. He delights in her growth of intellect, her growing charms, her newly acquired wit and blooming natural graces. Directing and watching her growth is a hobby for him; his primary interest is to be a successful businessman, well liked by all. Carrie is to him an object of pride or a project for satisfaction. Not once does he realize that she is far more spirited and sensitive and cleverer than he is.

Carrie knows full well that Drouet will not marry her. He is not a marrying man. Her conscience, as well as her growing self-esteem, requires that she find a man who is willing to marry her. She has been led by Hurstwood to believe that he is free to marry; whereas in reality he merely wishes to set her up in a South Side apartment as his mistress. Ironically, she finds her own justification for leaving Drouet in her knowledge that she will never be more than his mistress.

In addition to the possibility of finding honor and self-respect with Hurstwood, there is yet another reason for her attraction to him. This is the matter of sympathy which he arouses in her. Hurstwood realizes that Carrie is of a sympathetic nature and so with her he capitalizes upon this quality which he has found lacking in other women. Also, in extending toward Hurstwood her own sympathies in recompense for the lack of understanding and the indifference he meets in other people, she begins to see that she herself suffers the same plight. Yet Carrie is still naive enough to believe that Hurstwood loves her in the same manner in which she loves him.

Carrie, furthermore, is flattered that Hurstwood, "a man of the world," should find her, a shopgirl, so interesting and attractive. Hurstwood is an ideal figure to Carrie, a visitor from the "higher world" of wealth, power, and influence. She can hardly believe that Hurstwood is ready to invite her to join that higher world.

Irony, which might be defined as the difference perceived by the author and reader between the world of intention or desire and the real world, appears in various forms in these chapters. The point of Carrie's mistaken belief that Hurstwood is prepared to marry her has already been mentioned. There is an even deeper irony in Hurstwood's intended desire to keep his life uncomplicated and free of entanglements which would endanger his standing in the business and social community. When Carrie finally does "win" Hurstwood, it happens at the expense of his fine reputation and powerful influence.

There is dramatic irony in Drouet's unconscious commentary upon his own plight after the theater, when he says that a man should be more attentive to his wife if he wants to keep her.

Finally, ironic detail is used in these chapters. In the presence of Drouet, who once made her feel she had found a calm spot in a "sea of trouble," Carrie feels "all at sea mentally" when discussing Hurstwood. It is with a further ironic twist, then, that Carrie is shown wearing a "sailor hat" when she meets her new lover in the park in Chapter 15.

Dreiser continues to dramatize the theme of the editorial intrusion of Chapter 12. He is careful to show how words are often irrelevant to human situations; but he also wishes to demonstrate the paradoxical opposite of the idea—that is when a character seeks to find words to express his imagined subtlety of feeling, he begins to feel what has never existed until he described it: "Hurstwood surprised himself with his fluency.... He began to feel those subleties which he could find words to express. With every expression came increased conception."

 **CHAPTER 16**

## Summary

Drouet, having promised his lodge brothers that he would find an actress for their fund-raising theatrical, turns to Carrie as a last resort. After some coaxing she becomes very willing to try a part in the melodrama. Because the members of the lodge to which he belongs know he is not married, Drouet has Carrie's name listed on the program as "Carrie Madenda," explaining to her that this would be to her advantage if she doesn't "make a hit."

Carrie learns her part very quickly, immersing herself in its "sorrowful demeanor, the tremolo music, the long, explanatory cumulative addresses."

## Commentary

Carrie's imagination makes her suitable for an actress. She begins to learn her part avidly. Once again Dreiser uses the combined imagery of the rocking chair and the sea, in addition to the imagery of the theater: "As she rocked to and fro she felt the tensity of woe in abandonment, the magnificence of wrath after deception, the languor of sorrow after defeat. Thoughts of all the charming women she had seen in plays — every fancy, every illusion which she had concerning the stage — now came back as a returning tide after the ebb." For Carrie the world of the stage, like the world of her imagination, is the most real of all possible worlds.

## CHAPTERS 17-19

### Summary

During her next visit with Hurstwood, Carrie tells him all about her role in the forthcoming melodrama. He is pleased to learn that Carrie has capabilities and ambition. Hurstwood assures Carrie that he will contrive to keep Drouet from knowing that she told him about the theatrical. When Drouet does stop by at Fitzgerald and Moy's, Hurstwood remarks that they must give Carrie "a nice little send-off" and insists that Carrie and Drouet take supper with him after the play.

At the rehearsal, Carrie's natural acting ability is noticed by the director, who is surprised to learn that she has no stage experience. While Carrie rehearses, Hurstwood does not sit idle. He becomes a behind-the-scenes public relations man, taking every opportunity to publicize the show among his friends in the order, in which both he and Drouet are members.

Carrie is very nervous about the forthcoming performance, imagining all manners of horror and embarrassment if she fails to do well. Once she arrives at the theater, however, all the "nameless paraphernalia of disguise" transport her into a new and friendly atmosphere. Here she is part of the world of beautiful clothes, flowers, and elegant carriages. "She had come upon it as one who stumbles upon a secret passage, and, behold, she was in the chamber of diamonds and delight!" The gaslights, the makeup, and the costume transform Carrie into "Laura, the Belle of Society."

Hurstwood has enticed to the theater a host of gentlemen and their wives. Here, he is the star, the center of attraction: "It was greatness in a way, small as it was."

For a while, all of Carrie's earlier fears are realized; the performance of all the actors is terrible. As the female lead, Carrie seems the worst of all. As Drouet and Hurstwood sit nervously in their box, Hurstwood stares at Carrie onstage, "as if to hypnotize her into doing better." When Carrie exits, Drouet goes backstage to bolster her waning courage. Gradually she gains more confidence and moves onstage "with a steady grace, born of inspiration." Her performance moves the entire audience, but especially Drouet, who resolves to marry her, and Hurstwood, who becomes even more determined to take her from Drouet.

After the drama, Carrie is elated by her newfound powers. For once she looks down upon Hurstwood and not up at him. After the supper, she promises secretly to meet Hurstwood the next day and returns home with the enthusiastic Drouet.

## Commentary

In striving to show the workings of fate, Dreiser found it necessary to draw heavily from the well of unforeseen coincidence. Therefore, he inserts this theatrical episode where it is not entirely dramatically feasible but still necessary to his philosophy. Dreiser's view of life saw coincidence and external and unforeseeable incidents or episodes as a very real part of man's existence. Thus, he felt it quite relevant to introduce the Elks' benefit melodrama at this point. Despite the many new resolutions made by Drouet and Hurstwood, then, it appears to be part of Carrie's fate to become an actress, even if through the most curious sequence of causes.

In her brief taste of theatrical life, Carrie finds a sure way of climbing into the world of her imagination. Carrie is never so introspective as to inquire why "An Hour in Elf Land" holds such great appeal for her. Nevertheless, in her performance it is impossible to ignore the great changes that have come over the

48

young girl who climbed on the train from Columbia City. At that
time "she could scarcely toss her head gracefully"; now waiting
in the wings for her cue, she is encouraged by Drouet to "get
that toss" of her head that is characteristic of the Belle of Society.

The very world over which she reigns onstage is a pack of
"Siberian wolves," who move away from her scornfully as she
enters. Not only in the speeches themselves which she delivers
but also in their effect upon Drouet and Hurstwood there lies
much irony. Many of her speeches bear direct relevance to Carrie's situation—"it is a sad thing to want for happiness, but it
is a terrible thing to see another groping about blindly for it,
when it is almost within the grasp"; "my existence hidden from
all save two in the wide world, and making my joy out of that
innocent girl who will soon be his wife"; "her beauty, her wit,
her accomplishments, she may sell to you; but her love is the
treasure without money and without price."

In her role as Laura, Carrie is the woman damned by society,
yet desired by all, she is incapable of giving love. Laura remains
an outcast of the very society she rules. Surrounded by willing
lovers, clothed in finery, Laura will never be able to find love
or satisfaction. In the figure of Laura, there is the ironic foreshadowing of the popular famous actress, Miss Carrie Madenda.

## CHAPTERS 20-21

### Summary

On the morning after Carrie's performance, Hurstwood is
troubled with the problem of getting her away from Drouet.
Since both he and his wife are in a bad mood, they bicker over
family details. Mrs. Hurstwood is determined to receive more
"ladylike treatment" in the future.

Carrie is basking in the glory of her own achievement,
Hurstwood's passion for her forming a pleasant background. She
begins to feel the subtle change in feeling that transfers one from

the charity line into the ranks of almsgivers. Now she will dispense the favors.

Drouet is suddenly more attentive to Carrie and promises sincerely to marry her. He is beginning to sense her independence and hopes to avoid any possible danger.

Carrie leaves the house right after Drouet. Drouet, upon returning to retrieve some papers, finds the apartment empty, except for the chambermaid. As he flirts with the girl he learns that Hurstwood has been visiting Carrie nearly every day during his absence. Drouet broods upon this new information and resolves to "find out, b'George, whether she'll act that way or not."

Carrie and Hurstwood meet in the park once more. After much ado, Carrie consents to leave Drouet at the end of a week. Hurstwood agrees to marry her then: "He would promise anything, everything, and trust to fortune to disentangle him." Carrie begins to believe that she is actually in love with the man.

*Commentary*

These two very short chapters are used by Dreiser to build suspense. Their brevity suggests the emotional intensity in the situations of the three characters. Although the chapters are short, they are extremely important to the structure of the novel. Drouet begins to suspect Carrie's infidelity at nearly the same moment she resolves to leave him. In the intensity of the moment, Drouet forgets to maintain his beguiling charm with the chambermaid and Carrie forgets she is "married" to Drouet. Hurstwood, determined to have "Paradise, whatever might be the result," forgets to reason carefully. He lies and throws himself into the sea of his selfish passion.

Carrie, desiring marriage above all else, commits herself to Hurstwood on the very day that Drouet resolves to marry her. Hurstwood, promising marriage, is unaware of the danger that his wife is presently holding in store for him.

The imagery of the sea continues in the scene between Carrie and Hurstwood. (Compare this with the imagery of storms and upheaval in Chapter 22.) Hurstwood wants to "plunge in" and expostulate with Carrie, but finds himself "fishing for words." For Carrie the "floodgates" are open, and she finds herself "still illogically drifting and finding nothing at which to catch," "drifting . . . on a borderless sea of speculation." Hurstwood beats on against the current of Carrie's indecision. The imagery reveals Drouet's intention to show the nature of man's existence in a world of flux and irresistible change. Man is dominated and controlled by the forces of nature. At those times when he most needs it, his reason abandons him.

## CHAPTERS 22-23

### Summary

"The misfortune of the Hurstwood household was due to the fact that jealousy, having been born out of love, did not perish with it." Mrs. Hurstwood maintains a form of jealousy that turns itself into hatred. She is resentful and suspicious of Hurstwood as she observes his youthful demeanor.

Mrs. Hurstwood learns from the family doctor that Hurstwood had been driving recently on the Boulevard. Since she knows it was not their daughter Jessica who was with him and certainly not herself, she concludes that Hurstwood is seeing another woman.

The day after Carrie's theater appearance, Mrs. Hurstwood hears from a few acquaintances how sorry they were to learn she was "ill" and could not attend. She broods herself "into a state of sullen desire for explanation and revenge."

Hurstwood returns home from business in a sunny mood, hoping to improve relations somewhat with his wife. With a "wrathful sneer" Mrs. Hurstwood accuses him of "trifling around." It seems to Hurstwood that she knows much more about his recent activities then she reveals. As tempers flare,

Mrs. Hurstwood threatens to consult her lawyer and Hurstwood leaves the room.

Once again Carrie is fraught with doubt and indecision. Is it wise to leave the secure relationship she has with Drouet on the chance that Hurstwood will marry her?

Upon returning home that evening, Drouet begins to cross-examine Carrie about her relations with Hurstwood, revealing to her that Hurstwood is married. To his surprise Carrie attacks him for not warning her earlier about Hurstwood. The argument wavers back and forth until Drouet packs his clothes and leaves in a fit of jealous anger.

### Commentary

Dreiser shows in these chapters two of the ways in which jealousy manifests itself. Drouet's jealousy is in keeping with his penchant for fantasy and his blundering kindness. He seeks no revenge over Carrie; he is willing to accept her indiscretions, and when that becomes futile he shows a real concern for her welfare. But even as Carrie begins to consider it better to stay with Drouet rather than go with Hurstwood, a married man, Drouet's temper suddenly flares and he leaves, slamming the door. Carrie is astonished at the sudden rise of passion in the "good-natured and tractable" drummer. The narrator remarks that it is not possible for Carrie to see "the wellspring of human passion. A real flame of love is a subtle thing. It burns as a will-o'-the-wisp, dancing onward to fairylands of delight. It roars as a furnace. Too often jealousy is the quality upon which it feeds."

Mrs. Hurstwood's jealousy is of an entirely different type. It is not passionate and sudden as in Drouet. It is cold and calculated to produce harm. It is the result of her resentment of Hurstwood's charm and "the airy grace with which he still took the world." She is in search of the clear proof of "one overt deed" which will release her wrath. As she broods she becomes "impending disaster itself." When she attacks Hurstwood, she remains cool and cynical, "a pythoness in humor." In contrast to Drouet, who shows a concern for Carrie's welfare, Mrs. Hurstwood wishes to strangle and crush her husband. She will consider her revenge unfinished until this happens.

Dreiser draws his imagery in these two chapters from savage nature. The vision of doom finds expression in images of stormy weather and "blackening thunderclouds" pouring forth "a rain of wrath." In the tempest of his wife's savage jealousy, Hurstwood is "like a vessel, powerful and dangerous, but rolling and floundering without sail." Similarly, in the onslaught of Drouet's discovery about her and Hurstwood and her own discovery about Hurstwood's marriage, Carrie is shaken loose from her "mooring of logic" and becomes "an anchorless, storm-beaten little craft which could do absolutely nothing but drift." Through such imagery Dreiser demonstrates his "naturalistic" philosophy, showing his belief that man is merely an object battered about by the dark forces of the natural universe. The ship, a conventional image of man's temporary but heroic triumph over nature, is cast adrift and battered about mercilessly.

## CHAPTERS 24-25

### Summary

Hurstwood leaves his home to take a room in a hotel. Uncertain of what his wife will do next, he is forced into inaction. Mrs. Hurstwood, on the contrary, proceeds to press her advantage and begins to make heavy demands of money. Cursing himself for placing his property in her name some years ago, Hurstwood is further distressed by the possibility that she will carry news of his behavior to his employers. He turns from these thoughts to thoughts of Carrie, telling himself that she will wait for him.

In the morning he goes to his office to check the mail, dreading to hear from his wife but hoping to hear from Carrie. Next he goes to the park to wait for Carrie but she does not appear. As he mounts a streetcar, it begins to rain, which only adds to his distress. Once again he checks his mail. After lunch, a messenger arrives with a demand for money from Mrs. Hurstwood, but he sends the boy away with no reply. Later another demand arrives, threatening to expose him to Fitzgerald and Moy if he does not send the money asked.

Hurstwood decides to deliver the money himself, and takes a cab through the dreary rain only to find himself locked out of his own home. He returns dejectedly to his office.

In the meantime, he has received no word from Carrie and begins to suspect that perhaps she has heard all about him. All day his thoughts range back and forth between Carrie and his new problems. The weekend is spent in much "mental perturbation."

Monday's mail brings a letter from his wife's attorneys asking him to call. Hurstwood does not respond. On Tuesday he drives out to Carrie's apartment but leaves before seeing her because he thinks he is being followed.

On Wednesday another note from the attorneys reveals that Mrs. Hurstwood has begun divorce proceedings. Now Hurstwood knows what to expect. If he does not see the lawyers he will be sued for divorce promptly. If he does, he will "be offered terms that would make his blood boil."

*Commentary*

The presentation of these chapters resembles that of Chapter 4, wherein Carrie's grueling factory job is presented. Nearly every moment of time is registered both by the character and reader, with the result that time appears to be an endless progression of minute and distressing details. In his anxiety Hurstwood seems to be on the treadmill of his own destruction. He must do something or else "drift along to catastrophe."

Throughout the novel up to this point, Hurstwood has been characterized as a man of great persuasive qualities and power, but even he is laid low by the great demonic force of jealousy and revenge that drives his wife. Just as much as Drouet or Carrie, he is capable of being victimized by a set of circumstances beyond his control. Now, locked out of his own house, he sees that the power he had wielded there is lost to him.

The dreary rainy setting of Chapter 24 serves to put the images of storm and doom of the preceding chapters on an external plane. The "lowering clouds of suspicion" have produced a literal rain in which Hurstwood wanders back and forth from office to home. In addition, Hurstwood finds he must frequently wipe the moisture from his brow, a detail which is perhaps too literal.

It should be noted that here, precisely in the middle of the novel, the reader's attention has been drawn away from Carrie to Hurstwood. The story of Hurstwood's fall becomes inextricably connected with the story of Carrie's rise to eminence; the fate of one is entangled with the other. Appearing before only as a "minor" character, Hurstwood has become more and more conspicuous while Carrie is at times only mentioned as a background for Hurstwood's condition.

## CHAPTER 26

### Summary

The focus of the narrative shifts back to Carrie sitting alone in her rocking chair after Drouet's departure. She realizes that he may never return and so begins to formulate plans for the future. Certainly she cannot go to Hurstwood for aid, for she is shocked by the "evidence of human depravity" she sees in the man.

Pausing for a bite of food, Carrie begins to wonder how much money she has left. She discovers she has but seven dollars; however, the rent has been paid to the end of the month. She must leave the apartment then, for she cannot go on living with Drouet even if he did return.

On the next day, Friday, Carrie sets out to find work, but she must return home because of the same rain that dampened Hurstwood's spirits. Carrie visits a few shops on Saturday morning, discovering how her new appearance causes the men of business to be much more polite than they had been the previous winter. Nevertheless, she is determined not to take advantage of special favors and gives up the search for the time being.

Remembering Drouet's advice about going on the stage, she arises Monday morning and begins the round of theaters, looking for a small part. She meets two troupe managers, both of whom advise her that she must seek theatrical work in New York. That afternoon she drafts a letter to Hurstwood, telling him, "You have caused me more misery than you can think. I hope you will get over your infatuation for me. We must not meet any more."

The next morning she mails the letter and begins in vain to seek employment in the large department stores. While she is out, Drouet returns to make amends, but finding the apartment empty, he leaves. He does plan to return soon, however.

## Commentary

Carrie's search for a part in the theater is reminiscent of her earlier search for a factory job. The world of the theater is perhaps more hostile because the men she speaks to take liberties with her that the shopmen would not dare. To the shopmen she was a commodity; to the theater managers she is a toy or a source of low amusement.

Carrie's position is in many ways worse than it had been when she first came to the city. Then, there was always the opportunity to return to Columbia City or to seek momentary refuge with the Hansons. Now she can do neither. Her fascination and awe for the world of the theater is much greater than was her attraction to the business world. It seems foolhardy to her to think of trying the large theater companies. "Her spirits were materially reduced, owing to the newly restored sense of magnitude of the great interests and the insignificance of her claims upon society, such as she understood them to be."

## CHAPTER 27

*Summary*

Hurstwood spends the day thinking of his plight. Carrie no longer wants to see him. His wife is seeking to ruin him. What can he do?

Noticing that Drouet is now living at the Palmer House, Hurstwood rushes out to Carrie's apartment but finds she is not at home. He returns to the saloon and begins to imbibe more than is his custom. For a time he forgets his troubles and enjoys the society of wealthy friends and acquaintances. After the saloon closes, Hurstwood works in his office.

Checking the safe door, as is his nightly custom, Hurstwood is astonished to discover that it had not been locked and that about ten thousand dollars is in it. Before he shuts the safe he pauses to consider what it would be like to have so much ready cash. He could run off with Carrie and get rid of his wife. The liquor warms his imagination.

Hurstwood wavers back and forth for some time, removing the money, then replacing it, and removing it again and yet again. Suddenly, the lock snaps shut as he stands with the money in his hand. The indecision turns to action. Hurstwood stuffs the money into a satchel and rushes out. He takes a cab to Carrie's apartment and tells the servant girl to fetch Carrie because Drouet is in the hospital and wishes to see her. Carrie is so bewildered that she believes the story and the cab carries them off to the railroad terminal.

*Commentary*

Hurstwood attempts to solve his predicament in an action of the most crucial relevance. In dramatizing man's complete helplessness against the forces which control him, Dreiser's handling of the theft ranks among the most revealing scenes of all his work. The incident was so integral to his philosophy of life that with variations it appeared again twenty-five years later in the center of *An American Tragedy*. The perfect balance of motive and accident leads Hurstwood into committing a crime that will result in his own destruction. "When Waters Engulf Us We Reach for a Star," the title Dreiser assigns to this episode, expresses epigrammatically the clouding of intelligent self-interest in moments of panic by any apparent solution that suggests itself. For a brief moment, illusion overwhelms reality. A man takes one false step and his life is forfeit.

Intensely motivated by anger and by the impending scandal which threatens to cost him his managerial position, Hurstwood's balance is lost. Whether it is true that Hurstwood dominates *Sister Carrie*, stealing all attention from the title character, is a matter of dispute that can be settled only by personal taste. Dreiser does document the man's decline and fall in long and minutely detailed sequence, yet it is precisely through such extended contrast that the reader sees both Carrie and Hurstwood in a clear light. Both walk a tightrope in the precarious material world. One looks down and loses his balance, the other keeps her eyes on the tether ahead.

The central image of insecurity — Hurstwood's wavering between theft and resisted temptation — symbolizes the whole society that Dreiser evokes. It is a society in which there are no real equals, and no equilibrium, but only people moving up and down. As they waver back and forth — Carrie in her rocking chair, Hurstwood in front of the safe — they search in near hysteria for a way to the top.

## CHAPTERS 28-29

*Summary*

Hurstwood and Carrie board the Detroit train. When the train is out of Chicago Hurstwood admits that Drouet's injury was merely a ruse to get Carrie to go away with him. She makes an effort to get away from Hurstwood but his pleadings and explanations make her reconsider. She is drawn by his daring and power and is flattered by the thought that he has left Chicago to be with her. Carrie is once again struck by indecision, but decides in favor of Hurstwood when he offers to marry her.

From Detroit the couple continue in a sleeping car to Montreal, where they register in a hotel under the name of "G. W. Murdock and wife." In the lobby of the hotel Hurstwood experiences the first of a series of encounters with his past life in Chicago, a stockbroker named Mr. Kenny. The fear of being discovered causes him to decline Kenny's invitation to breakfast with him. Next he spies a man who seems to be a private detective and concludes that Montreal is too warm for him. He plans to move to New York because "its mysteries and possibilities of mystification" are "infinite."

Hurstwood reads the local papers, wherein is published an account of his misdeeds, and he regrets his terrible error. A knock at the door reveals a Chicago detective who threatens him with exposure and arrest if he does not return the money. Hurstwood corresponds with Fitzgerald and Moy, with the result that he repays $9,500 and keeps $1,300 as a "loan." Carrie, of course, is ignorant of the whole affair.

The couple are married illegally under the name of Wheeler, "by a Baptist minister, the first divine they found convenient." The newlyweds board the New York train and arrive the next morning. Carrie, who is beginning "to have a few opinions of her own," does not like New York after her first impression.

*Commentary*

After the theft, Hurstwood becomes a different man. He has lost his identity in the world of Chicago society. Without his managerial position, family, or property, he is simply another fugitive from the law, a creature driven by instinct and fantasy, haunted by misgivings. It seems a blow to Hurstwood that the detective who tracks him down is only of the "lowest stratum welcomed at the resort." He himself is a thief and a safecracker, or so the newspapers say. Reading his own description in the newspaper, Hurstwood realizes the nature of social injustice which sees only one side of a tragedy. The newspapers report only that he stole the money. How and why were only matters of indifferent speculation. All the complications which preceded the theft are unknown. "He was accused without being understood."

As the train rolls onward from Chicago, the relationship between Carrie and Hurstwood changes dramatically. Carrie realizes that she does not love the man, but sees in him the only way out of a desperate situation. No longer is she so fascinated by Hurstwood that she responds automatically to his every wish. She will have her way; she is nominally free to leave him if she wishes, yet she has the apparent security of marriage.

Throughout these chapters Dreiser repeats the idea that the very motion of travel has a deep psychological effect. The progress of the train is an important factor in Carrie's decision to remain with Hurstwood. "The speeding wheels and disappearing country put Chicago farther and farther behind." Dreiser opens Chapter 29, "The Solace of Travel: The Boats of the Sea," with a discussion of travel. To the untraveled, new places are fascinating. Travel "solaces and delights." New things and places to see are so fascinating that they cannot be neglected, and the mind, "which is a mere reflection of sensory impressions, succumbs to the flood of objects." One forgets lovers, puts aside sorrow, and suspends impending problems. Thus Carrie is fascinated by her entry into New York with its boats and highways, and especially the East River, "the first sign of the great sea."

## CHAPTERS 30-31

### Summary

Approximately the first two years in New York is sketched in briefly. Hurstwood purchases a one-third partnership in a downtown establishment, one not nearly so "swell" as Fitzgerald and Moy's. After a few months, business improves and Hurstwood begins to resume his old public self. He occasionally gambles and attends the theater with friends but cherishes his home life greatly. He begins to enlarge his wardrobe, but does not encourage Carrie to do so. It seems to him that she is content to be a housewife and so he begins to relax his demeanor before her and treat her with "easy familiarity."

For Carrie the routine of running the flat and basking in Hurstwood's affection seem interesting for a time. She attempts to understand that Hurstwood must spend his money frugally and so makes no demands for luxuries or entertainment. Because she is "passive and receptive" and she does not love Hurstwood, she is not jealous of his public life. Gradually, however, she becomes aware of the changes in Hurstwood and begins to resent being neglected.

In the second year, Carrie meets a new neighbor, Mrs. Vance, whose elegant clothing and fashionable behavior begin to awaken her old desires. One day she attends a matinee with Mrs. Vance, and she becomes fascinated with the "showy parade" of "pretty faces and fine clothes" on Broadway. "With a start she awoke to find that she was in fashion's crowd, on parade in a show place—and such a show place!" Carrie is "cut to the quick" by her own lack of quality and stylish apparel and she resolves never to walk upon Broadway again until she looks better. She feels her old desire to enter into the world of fashion as an equal; "then she would be happy!"

## Commentary

The treatment of passing time in these chapters, in contrast to the plodding sequences of the last days in Chicago or the hectic compressed time of the departure and trip through Canada, is leisurely and without incident. Nearly two years pass by in New York, whereas before only about six months had elapsed since Carrie's arrival in Chicago. Such a treatment of time reveals the routine existence into which Carrie and Hurstwood have entered. Nothing much happens and so time passes unnoticed.

Credit must be given Hurstwood for his serious attempt to forestall the tragedy of disappearing into the walls of New York. In contrast to Chicago, where celebrities were so few, New York is full of notables and a man of Hurstwood's fallen station and age has no chance of gaining prestige. In New York, the origin of all "wealth, place, and fame," Hurstwood finds himself in the humiliating situation of searching for work and living on a frugal budget. He lives in constant fear of the shame that would come in meeting old friends.

Unfortunately, Hurstwood takes Carrie for granted. Struggling with his own problems, he is unaware that she requires more than mere affection, mortgaged furniture, and the vague promise of more money in the future. "He failed therein to take account of the frailties of human nature—the difficulties of matrimonial life." Dreiser makes frequent mention of the fact that no great bond of love exists to hold the couple together. Both go on, unaware and unadvised of the problems and requirements of the other. Neither has enough faith to invite the other into full confidence. Hurstwood lives in the frustration of the past and Carrie lives in the fantasies of the future.

Hurstwood draws contentment from his mistaken belief that Carrie is content with her lot, but as Carrie sees more and more of New York, her early desires and frustrations are reawakened. Once again she feels herself cut off from Hurstwood's world, as well as the higher world beyond him.

In Hurstwood's attentive behavior toward Mrs. Vance, Carrie perceives the changes that have come over their relationship. She begins to feel stale and gloomy and begins to think of old possibilities. "There were no immediate results to this awakening, for Carrie had little power of initiative; but, nevertheless, she seemed ever capable of getting herself into the tide of change where she would be easily borne along."

In invoking the past and omitting any specific reference to the future, Dreiser succeeds in building a kind of suspense. By pointing out the recurrent parallel patterns of change in Carrie and Hurstwood, the author invites the reader to speculate about "future possibility."

## CHAPTER 32

*Summary*

After the matinee Carrie returns home to dwell upon what seems to her the extraordinarily beautiful world of the theater and regrets in her heart that she cannot be part of it. Nevertheless, New York seems to be a place filled with even more wonder and fantasy than Chicago itself. She believes that she can "never live" until she becomes a part of New York society.

When Hurstwood enters, Carrie is in her rocking chair, moody, testy, and resentful of having her reveries broken in upon. He invites her to the theater with him that same evening and she accepts.

About a month later, Carrie goes out for dinner and theater as the guest of the Vances and Mrs. Vance's cousin, Bob Ames. As they dine at Sherry's, a very exclusive restaurant of the period, Ames, a "clear-eyed, fine-headed youth," suggests to Carrie that wealth and fashionable attire are only unnecessary luxuries. Ames seems "wiser than Hurstwood, saner and brighter than Drouet." His sincere rejection of excessive wealth removes some of the bitterness of the contrast between the society life and Carrie's life. Yet Carrie is attracted by his intelligence, and sees that his "calm indifference" is not the response of a bitter loser. When the evening is over Carrie retires to her rocking chair to think over the events of the day. "Through a fog of longing and conflicting desires....she was beginning to see."

*Commentary*

Ever since leaving Chicago, Carrie has desired little in the way of entertainment and worldly possessions. It is an inexplicable quirk of character, yet one of which even Carrie herself is not aware. Dreiser has prepared the reader for a revelation on

Carrie's part for several chapters through his choice of imagery and detail and the carefully delineated presentation of the "love" between Carrie and Hurstwood, and especially through his handling of time. Since her afternoon with Mrs. Vance, Carrie has been experiencing the aftereffects of "the great awakening blow." Even if she retreats briefly from her reveries, she will return to them again: "Time and repetition—ah, the wonder of it! The dropping water and the solid stone—how utterly it yields at last!"

Mrs. Vance, who has become Carrie's fashion adviser, just as Drouet had been, is eager to show Carrie the ways of the higher world. Yet her plan backfires because her own cousin, Bob Ames, invites Carrie to question seriously the values and assumptions she has held. Ames is happy and successful, even though he is all alone. Indeed, wonders Carrie, why can't I reach my goals alone? Why not try to find a part in the theater? At the "feast of Belshazzar" the handwriting on the wall becomes clear with Ames as the seer. Suddenly, after three years of being a mere housewife to the tired Hurstwood, Carrie is beginning to see that the possibilities of New York exist for her only if she is willing to take advantage of them.

Realizing that not only Hurstwood, but she herself, has become rather dull and uninteresting, Carrie is now on the verge of turning her imaginary world of the theater into a reality. The water is striking through the stone at last.

## CHAPTERS 33-35

*Summary*

Even though she does not see Ames again for some time, Carrie thinks of him as an ideal to contrast other men by. Compared to the youthful Ames, Hurstwood seems old and uninteresting, while Drouet seems foolish and shallow.

Hurstwood himself is sliding past the prime of life, and largely because of that, he begins to lose the decisiveness that had once made him prosperous and successful. For a time this is not apparent even to him, but gradually he begins to see himself outside "the walled city" of youth and easy money and fine clothes.

The narrator postulates that this change for the worse is the result of "certain poisons in the blood, called katastates." The poisons arising from remorse work against the system and finally produce "marked physical deterioration." Subject to these, Hurstwood becomes a brooder.

Reading the daily newspaper reports of the celebrities with whom he used to associate, Hurstwood becomes even more depressed with his own lowly state. In an effort to avert disaster, Hurstwood decides that he and Carrie should move into a smaller apartment and dismiss the maid. Carrie is very gloomily affected by the change, "more seriously than anything that had yet happened." She begins to recall that Hurstwood "had practically forced her to flee with him."

As Hurstwood continues to brood, only the newspapers and his own thoughts seem of any importance to him. "The delight of love had again slipped away." To make matters worse, the lease on the Warren Street establishment expires and Hurstwood finds himself facing the coming winter without any income. He begins to search halfheartedly for a new position. He visits a few saloons but realizes that his meager $700 is not nearly enough for a substantial investment.

Hurstwood's appearance is still excellent, however; he continues to dress well and looks prosperous. Now forty-three years old and "comfortably built" he finds walking about the city makes his legs tired, his shoulders ache, and his feet hurt. It makes him bitter to have to enter business places announcing that he was looking for "something to do."

His days are largely spent lounging in the lobbies of the larger New York hotels watching the world pass before him. At night he returns home to read the papers and lose himself in the "Lethean waters . . . of telegraphed intelligence." So he reads and rocks himself in the warm room near the radiator.

The routine he falls into consists of reading the morning newspapers, leaving the house in search of work only to rest in a hotel lobby, and returning home to read the evening papers. As winter sets in he leaves the house even less, except to go on household errands as a means of justifying his presence. He deteriorates quickly, wearing his worst clothes, and shaving only once a week. His very appearance becomes revolting to Carrie, and she begins to sleep alone.

By doing all the daily errands, Hurstwood cuts household expenses to a minimum and never gives any money to Carrie. When he is not out buying food or coal, he sits by the radiator, reading and rereading his newspaper.

## Commentary

Dreiser suggests in one of his many editorial asides that Hurstwood's failing condition is the universal lot of men. After a certain time the balance of youth and age begins to tip in favor of age. The body and mind lose their vitality. Therefore Hurstwood suddenly finds himself an outsider to the small circumscribed world to which he used to belong. The realization of this removes him even farther.

Hurstwood still believes that by economizing severely for a year so that he can reinvest, he and Carrie can rise again to a state of financial well-being. Unfortunately, he is fooling himself. He begins to forget how sullen and depressed he has become so that everything he tries is doomed to failure.

By showing Hurstwood going through almost exactly the same motions as Carrie as he searches for work, Dreiser underscores his philosophy of fate and fortune. Through a few incidental changes, as they are altered and increased by time, Hurstwood has slipped from very high on his own social ladder to a point below the register. Like Carrie had been, he is forced to walk the streets and realize his own inexperience in the ways of the working world. He has few skills, for his past career was built upon his excellent appearance and jovial personality. He is forced to consider any opportunity that gives him "something to do."

As Hurstwood slips down into decadence, Carrie becomes more and more independent and detached from him. She does not fall with him but remains a "soldier of fortune," somehow believing that fate, even though it ruins Hurstwood, will provide for her. She continues to believe that the theater is a possible way out of the situation for her.

The parallels between Hurstwood and the Carrie of old suggest how different both have become. Now it is Hurstwood who sits idly rocking back and forth in the chair. His newspapers serve to banish the worries of the day. So far removed is he from the world of society, that it becomes a dream world, a land of fantasy where he flees to forget his troubles.

As Hurstwood sits daily in the Broadway hotel lobbies, he recalls how he used to be an important member of the clan of idle and gay people and reminisces bitterly how much money it takes to live in that manner. As he sits in one of the many plush lobbies, Hurstwood is approached by Mr. Cargill of Chicago. When Carrie made her debut in the Elks' theatrical three years ago, Cargill took advantage of the situation to introduce his wife and shake the hand of the influential and powerful Hurstwood. How clear and yet how far away that event seems to Hurstwood. Both men are now embarrassed by Hurstwood's obviously fallen condition.

In Chicago Carrie had nowhere to go but up. In New York, approaching age and constant depression make it possible for Hurstwood to go nowhere but down. He is now the walking shell of the man he used to be. Carrie cannot fully comprehend the changes in Hurstwood, for she does not know what it means to be completely without hope. As Hurstwood's respect for himself vanishes, it perishes for him in Carrie. She knows that he still has some money left and presentable clothes and that he is not unattractive when dressed up. She does not forget her own difficult struggle in Chicago, but neither does she forget that she never ceased trying to find work. It seems to her that Hurstwood never tried. He does not even consult the employment notices anymore. What Carrie does not understand is what Hurstwood understands too well: that a middle-aged man in a state of depression and without skills has no chance of finding work in New York when 80,000 people are unemployed.

Finally her patience and understanding reach the breaking point. When Hurstwood reminds her how expensive is the butter that she uses to flavor their meager half-pound of steak, she remarks archly, "You wouldn't mind if you were working." All feeling between them has perished and so Carrie begins to sleep alone, for the marriage bed no longer offers the mutual respect and understanding that it should.

## CHAPTER 36

### Summary

Although Carrie has avoided Mrs. Vance since she and Hurstwood have moved to the commonplace Thirteenth Street address, she experiences mixed feelings when she meets the young woman on the street by chance one day. She invites Mrs. Vance to visit "some time," afraid to have her see Hurstwood in his bedraggled condition.

Hurstwood, however, does not always sit about with his four-day beard and in a condition of "utmost nonchalance." Occasionally, he shaves and dresses merely to wander about the city. At times he joins in a poker game, neither winning nor losing significantly. One day he wins a few dollars, and the dim phantom of hope draws him back for another game the next day. Hurstwood is so keen to win, however, that his facial expressions give him away. He loses over sixty precious dollars. He resolves to play no more.

He continues to sit about the house, lacking pride or interest in his own or Carrie's welfare. While Carrie is out one day, Mrs. Vance stops to visit and is dismayed by Hurstwood's appearance. An argument ensues when Carrie learns of this. Hurstwood is ashamed of himself; he dresses carefully and leaves the house. After treating himself to an expensive dinner, he decides to try his hand at another poker game. This time he loses nearly a hundred dollars.

Wondering what is becoming of himself, he wavers between extreme frugality and ridiculous self-indulgence. When it comes time to pay the rent, Hurstwood discovers that he is "nearing his last hundred dollars."

## Commentary

The significance of this chapter lies in the irony of Hurstwood's attempt to make money by playing poker. Through a series of chance occurrences combined with a certain ineptitude in responding wisely to these occurrences, Hurstwood has lost at the game of life. It is no wonder, then, that he fails so miserably at this backroom game of chance. Making the irony particularly incisive is the fact that while Hurstwood was prosperous and important, he had no difficulty in manipulating a game of euchre for Carrie to win. Now himself a pawn of fate, Hurstwood cannot believe that he has lost his skill at poker. Hurstwood does not "introspect"; consequently he fails to see that he is not "the old Hurstwood—only a man arguing with a divided conscience and lured by a phantom." He is no longer a master of the bluff. Carrie learns this shortly before he does himself.

Each chapter in the story of Hurstwood's dissolution is also a chapter in the tale of Carrie's disillusionment. In each chapter she learns a new lesson or discovers something new about her relationship with Hurstwood. In this episode she discovers that her "marriage" is not legal or binding. It does not exist; like "Murdock," "Wheeler," or even Hurstwood, it is merely one more trumped-up phantom of belief. When Hurstwood leaves the apartment, Carrie thinks for a moment that he is gone for good. This does not distress her; still dependent upon him for financial support, she is merely concerned that he has left her without money.

### CHAPTERS 37-39

*Summary*

As in Chicago, the idea of working in the theater comes to Carrie as a last resource in distress. One morning over breakfast she announces her intention of finding a job. Hurstwood is secretly afraid that she will become successful and desert him. He does not understand Carrie's mental ability; he does not realize that a person can be "emotionally — instead of intellectually — great."

To prevent Carrie from making any definite plans, Hurstwood lies that he anticipates obtaining a hotel job through an old friend and that he is beginning to hear from his "contacts" once more. He reflects that Carrie might work for a while until the job materializes.

Searching for work one day, Carrie returns with a copy of the *Clipper*, wherein are listed the names and addresses of the New York theatrical agents. Hurstwood picks a few at random and Carrie visits them to no avail, for minimal experience and a cash deposit are required before an agent will consider managing a young actress. Carrie decides to see the theater managers directly.

As she stops at various theaters of the city, Carrie must deal with all sorts of self-important types, from pompous doormen and box-office clerks to the "lords" themselves of these little businesses. All expect her to be very humble, and they resent her small intrusion upon their precious time. Finally, the manager of the Casino tells Carrie to return the following week, at which time there may be an opening in the chorus line.

When the week of waiting is over, Carrie returns to the Casino theater, where she is told to report the next morning for rehearsal. As the girl walks homeward, her delight turns to dissatisfaction with Hurstwood, whose "handicap of age" she does not comprehend.

Once again taking the name Carrie Madenda, the young chorine works hard at rehearsal everyday, "the sound of glory ringing in her ears." It seems to Carrie that Hurstwood has decided to sit about the house waiting for her to bring home her weekly twelve dollars. This annoys her, because she is anxious to buy new clothes with her salary.

Hurstwood stays home the night of the opening performance. The play is a hit and Carrie is assured of work for some time.

As Carrie works hard at the theater, Hurstwood sits home for a month reading the newspaper, his determination to seek work overclouded more and more by the conviction "that each particular day was not the day." Laying aside a few dollars for shaves and carfare, he announces to Carrie that he is finally out of money. Now the two are wholly dependent upon her for subsistence. When Hurstwood does "borrow" money for household expenses, he always returns the exact change to Carrie.

At the theater, Carrie makes friends with Lola Osborne, a "little gaslight soldier." The two spend much of their free time together looking for new work and shopping.

The theater manager and the ballet master agree that Carrie is a much better dancer than the average run of the girls and put her in charge of a "line," raising her salary to eighteen dollars. Nevertheless, after buying a few things for herself Carrie discovers again and again that she simply cannot support two people.

Carrie takes advantage of every opportunity to be out of the house away from Hurstwood, who makes mild and ineffectual protests against her absence. This only serves to widen the gap between them. While Carrie is visiting Lola one afternoon, two of the young lady's gentlemen admirers stop by to take her for a drive. Carrie is persuaded to join them and naturally forgets to return home in time to cook dinner for Hurstwood. As he sits home, grumbling to himself that Carrie is getting ahead now and he is "out of it," Carrie dines at the famed Delmonico's restaurant. The setting reminds her of the time she dined with the Vances and Bob Ames, whose ideals "burned in her heart." A sense of obligation forces her to go home directly after the performance, and so she must decline the offer of the youths to continue the day's festivities.

### Commentary

One of the major ironies, or reversals, of the novel arises from Carrie's desperate decision to become an actress. Up until now she had considered the theater only a part of her impossible fantasy world. The stage was "a door through she might enter that gilded state which she had so much craved."

As a "soldier of fortune," Carrie had always accepted the dictates of fate without question. She had been content to remain passive as Drouet or Hurstwood presided over her actions and provided financial security. Now that Hurstwood is unable to provide, he is also unable to direct Carrie's behavior. At this point, the brutal reality of starvation and the omnipresent fantasy of the theater converge to provide a course of action for the "little soldier."

The world in which she imagines herself is far less removed from the real world than are the realms of fantasy she has previously visited. Poverty and the fear of starvation make it a necessity for her to take a part in a Broadway show. She must go to the theater every evening to apply her makeup. After each performance she sees the elegant carriages waiting about with amorous youths in them seeking her attention. In just a short time, she will enjoy a generous income and will be able to buy the clothes she desires. As her mind wanders over these fantasies, Hurstwood's dreary state makes their beauty "more and more vivid." As the beauty of the fantasy become more vivid, it also becomes more and more realistic. For once, Carrie's fantasies do not fade; instead, the conditions of the world change, allowing them to become actual.

In Dreiser's world view such a drastic change in conditions is part of the ordinary flux of life. At one moment Carrie drifts along on a tempestuous sea; the next moment she finds herself on the crest of a wave riding toward success. Looking over her shoulder, she sees Hurstwood slipping beneath the stormy surface.

Dreiser never chose his details without great care. The publication *Clipper*, although it momentarily sets Carrie off on an uncertain course through the offices of Mrs. Bermudez and other theatrical agents, ultimately does provide her with the determination to stop at the port of the Casino theater.

Suggestions of the eternal sea of flux upon which the drama unfolds continue to appear in the minutest details. The very name "Carrie" suggests the girl's relation to the workings of fate. Similarly, "Madenda," coming from a Latin root meaning "wet" or "soaked," continues to enforce the imagery.

As Carrie's fortunes rise steadily, Hurstwood continues to become more defeated and bitter. Every minor advance for Carrie becomes a major setback for him, until finally he comes to blame Carrie for his own dissolution. He believes that Carrie is now satisfied and content with her lot and that her success will go to her head. Even as he sits brooding over this, however, Carrie sits with her friend Lola and two gallants, thinking not of her financial success or popularity, but of the emotional fulfillment that comes with being a good actress. The ideals of Bob Ames burn in her heart. It is not for Carrie to be content with the present; she forces herself always to look to the future for satisfaction.

## CHAPTERS 40-41

### Summary

The remainder of the summer and the autumn pass. Carrie obtains another part at a higher salary when the opera in which she played a part goes on the road. Hurstwood continues to sit in the rocking chair, reading his newspaper, promising himself that things will go better for him. Of course, the hotel job he talked about never materializes.

One winter day, after Carrie complains to Hurstwood that she cannot possibly pay all their bills by herself, Hurstwood reads an advertisement in the newspaper announcing that because of a labor strike, a Brooklyn trolley line is seeking motormen and conductors. Although his sympathy lies with the strikers, he decides to go to Brooklyn to find work because Carrie seems to suspect him of stealing her money.

Making his way through the cold to the trolley yard, he offers his services. The manager of the line is so pressed for workers that he decides to hire and train Hurstwood as a motorman. After a day of instruction and a cold night in the loft of the car storage barn, Hurstwood begins his first day of work in many months. The hours are long and the weather is cold, but the hardest and most dangerous part of the job is facing the angry strikers. Although there are policemen aboard the car for protection, Hurstwood is attacked and dragged off in a skirmish. He is finally rescued by the policemen, but as he is climbing back aboard the car, he is struck by a bullet.

The violence and the misery are too much for Hurstwood and he leaves nervously. After a long walk in the snow, he arrives home, tends to the slight wound he has received in the arm, and settles down comfortably to read his paper with relief.

### Commentary

Even though the reader has had mixed feelings about Hurstwood up to this point, the events of the Brooklyn episode are enough to compel anyone to feel sympathy for the man. Hurstwood seems selfish and stuffy until he is shown trying to deal with the impossible situation he faces. His sympathy lies with the striking workmen, for he knows what it is never to have enough money to survive, yet the strike offers him an opportunity to prove to Carrie and himself that he is "not down yet," that there must be something he could do.

Furthermore, Hurstwood is no longer as robust and alert as he used to be, and the cold and danger would be sufficient to dissuade a much younger man from attempting to operate a streetcar under such conditions. As he sets out for the yard in Brooklyn, he gains for a while some of the dignity of the old Hurstwood. He seems to possess a "shrewd and pleasant strength." Those conditions do not prevail for long, however; for when the manager of the trolley line asks, "What are you—a motorman?" he is forced to answer, "No; I'm not anything." Hurstwood's reply is a response to much more than the simple question. In his own eyes he is nothing but the ghost of what he once had been.

A charge often laid against naturalistic authors is that they often present factual or social data to achieve the "reality" of actual life and conditions without properly integrating such material into the structure of the novel. Although Dreiser's theories frequently caused him to view life as a series of unexpected events, the charge does not apply in this case. Hurstwood has for some time been reading about the unemployment situation in the city. By his own standards he is unemployable. Nevertheless, in times of strife and strike a job-seeker and a labor-seeker must both alter their standards. It is only a combination of the prevalence of unemployment and the occurrence of a strike that will provide the situation in which Hurstwood is able to force himself to try anything.

Dreiser combines the naturalist's talent for rendering the social phenomenon known as the labor strike with the artist's conception of structural development and character portrayal. The strike episode, then, is not only an accurate rendering of a strike but also a very integral part of the story of Hurstwood and Carrie.

As Carrie actually entered the fantasy world of the stage, so does Hurstwood enter for a while his own fantasy world of newspaper headlines; but, unlike Carrie, he fails to make a place for himself in his own world. The indignity and fear he experiences are too harsh for the faltering Hurstwood. "The real

thing was slightly worse than thoughts of it had been." As Carrie
rises, Hurstwood descends, and together their individual stories
comprise the plot of *Sister Carrie*.

   In contrast to Carrie's new clothing, which makes her part
of her new world, Hurstwood's clothing is now threadbare and
worn. It is not sufficiently warm for him to weather the cold
winter. The incongruity of a trolley motorman in worn gentle-
man's garb reveals Hurstwood's inability to cope with the world
changing about him. Clothing reveals the complete inversion of
the "marriage" of Carrie and Hurstwood. A few short years ago
he was the struggling breadwinner who occasionally indulged
himself in new clothing to meet the world, while Carrie
remained home, running the household in her outdated garb.
Now, however, Carrie is the hard-working breadwinner. She
buys new dresses in order to be a more complete part of the
world luck and fate have brought to her. It is Hurstwood who
stays home now. It is he who dresses poorly, and when he is not
immersed in his fantasies, he fetches the groceries and deals
with the tradesmen. The original relationship between them has
been totally inverted.

## CHAPTER 42

### Summary

   Carrie misunderstands Hurstwood's Brooklyn trolley
venture, thinking that "he had encountered nothing worse than
the ordinary roughness." The same night that Hurstwood spends
in the car barn Carrie gains the approval of the star of the show
through a clever ad lib remark. The line remains in the show,
and soon thereafter she wins her first speaking part.

   Having now "tried and failed," Hurstwood sinks lower and
begins to experience reveries of glorious past times when he
was the center of attention in Chicago society. He is continually
harassed at home by creditors.

   As Carrie's salary increases, so does her resentment at having to support Hurstwood's deadweight. She debates leaving

him to take a room with Lola Osborne. When a new part is given to her, she spends for costumes all the rent money she has been saving. The thought of leaving the pathetic Hurstwood fills her with sadness; nevertheless, one spring day she gathers her clothes and belongings and leaves the apartment. In a note to Hurstwood, she explains that she needs all the money she makes for clothes and costumes and that it is no use trying to keep up the flat. She gives him twenty dollars and all their furniture.

When Hurstwood returns after a day of wandering, he reads the note and is struck by a powerful sensation of coldness. He sits in the rocker for a long time, staring at the floor.

### Commentary

A counterpoint to the ebbing Hurstwood's pathetic answer— "No; I'm not anything"—is Carrie's clever remark to the star of the show one evening. Part of a group of Oriental beauties in a comic opera, she is led before the potentate, who asks, "Well, who are you?" Her answer, "I am yours truly," rocks the audience with appreciative laughter. Compared to Hurstwood's tight-lipped admission of defeat, Carrie's is a sign of her growing belief in herself and in her blossoming talents. Carrie, although she is somewhat timid, is a very capable young lady. She has learned much by experience.

Among the things she has learned is the manner in which to treat men. "No longer the lightest word of a man made her head dizzy. She had learned that men could change and fail." She is no longer won over through personal flattery. To win her over now a man must show the "kindly superiority" that Bob Ames had shown.

Through frequent reference to Ames, Dresier reminds the reader that Carrie is capable of a purely emotional and mental response to a man without overtones of materialistic desire. Unfortunately for her, however, Ames has forgotten her and is working faraway in another city. The one man who can move her is lost to her. With characteristic irony Dreiser reveals that life for Carrie is largely the process of substituting one form of desire and frustration for another.

Hurstwood does move her slightly, but he also repels her. Just before Carrie leaves him, she feels guilty and begins to act solicitously toward him. He is no longer worthless or shiftless to her, but run down and "beaten by chance." His eyes are no longer sharp and keen; his hair is beginning to turn gray; his hands are flabby and his face shows great wear. Perhaps, she thinks, his failure is not all his own fault. Nevertheless, he is still a burden to her and she resolves to leave him.

### CHAPTERS 43-44

*Summary*

When she first leaves Hurstwood, Carrie fears that he may wait around for her at the theater, but as the days pass she forgets him. "In a little while she was, except for occasional thoughts, wholly free of the gloom with which her life had been weighed in the flat." Now the "showy world" of the theater absorbs her interest.

As time passes, Carrie continues to receive larger and more attractive roles. Her photograph is published in a Sunday paper and she receives occasional notices.

Although her salary has been increased, Carrie finds that she is still as far removed as ever from the upper strata of society. Those who amiably approach her are interested only in their own pleasure; their advances lack any promise of genuine friendship.

Carrie's part as a pert, frowning Quakeress in a summer production at the Casino theater is the chief attraction of the play. One critic, musing about the unpredictability of public taste, writes, "The vagaries of fortune are indeed curious." Another coins the catch phrase, "If you wish to be merry, see Carrie frown." The manager of the theater and the author of the play send her congratulatory messages. Her salary is increased once again, this time to the incredible sum of one hundred and fifty dollars a week. Carrie finds that she has more money than she could possibily spend.

In a third-rate hotel downtown, Hurstwood reads of Carrie's successes and recognizes that she is now in "the walled city." She has become a celebrity of the sort he used to know so well. With a last gesture of pride, he resolves never to bother her.

The manager of a brand new hotel offers to Carrie a suite overlooking Broadway at a greatly reduced rate. The young star moves in with her friend Lola. The wealthy Mrs. Vance pays her a visit.

For a time Carrie enjoys the life of a popular young celebrity. She receives love letters and proposals from rich men, which she ignores. She is asked to perform at benefits. A young author seeks her out to show her his script. All the time, however, her understanding that she has not found "the door to life's perfect enjoyment" continues to grow. Carrie finds that there is nothing that she does which she really enjoys, and she begins to grow weary of such a life.

### Commentary

There are at least three different versions of the story of Carrie's sudden popularity. First, there is the public story blurted out in press releases and critical reviews. Next, there is Hurstwood's view that Carrie is selfish and has entered the "walled city" of wealth and influence, purposely leaving him outside the gate. Finally, there is Carrie's own ambivalent version. She is thrilled by her own talent and success and justifiably proud of the notice she receives. Yet, even as her income and popularity increase, she discovers more and more that the real world of eminence is an illusory place that is never "here," but always someplace above her or sometime in the future. She feels severely limited by her own judgment and intelligence, desiring to be serious like Bob Ames and wishing to be divorced from the heady world of theatrical comedy and pretense.

Carrie realizes that no one except Lola is actually interested in her. The world, she discovers, is very much like Drouet and Hurstwood. It merely wishes to amuse itself at her expense, regardless of the consequences. It is a world full of strangers out for all they can get.

Everything seems "rosy and bright" when Carrie receives her first large salary payment and she remembers how difficult it was when she worked in the miserable shoe factory in Chicago. Yet it is not long before the newly won money reveals its own "impotence," for Carrie's desires are now "in the realm of affection." At times it seems that not only Carrie but Dreiser as well is confused about what her desires really are: at one moment Carrie's foremost wish is for "affection," but a few sentences later it is revealed that Carrie must have more money. "If she wanted to do anything better or move higher she must have more — a great deal more."

It is a matter for speculation whether the Hotel Wellington, in which Carrie is installed, is the same hotel that Hurstwood spoke about in connection with a job. Whether it is, is actually unimportant, for the extravagance of the place is the important thing. The Wellington is the kind of hotel that Hurstwood used to lounge in while he pretended to seek work. Now Carrie resides in its opulent luxury and warmth, far removed from the struggles on the street below. Hurstwood has moved into a "third-rate . . . moth-eaten hotel"; to him, any decent hotel seems a "walled city."

## CHAPTER 45

*Summary*

Hurstwood spends the summer and fall moving about the lower part of the city, drifting from one cheap hotel to another. Finally, when he has spent all the money he received for the furniture in the apartment, he walks to a large Broadway hotel to find a job. His story interests the sympathetic manager, who gives him work as an odd-jobs man and a place to sleep. He must take orders from cooks, porters, and firemen. On an errand one February day, he gets a thorough soaking and chill which result in pneumonia. Until the following May, he recuperates at Bellevue Hospital.

Hoping to meet Carrie outside the theater one evening, Hurstwood misses his chance to see her when she arrives suddenly and rushes inside. With an aching stomach and sore feet, he joins a group of fellow unfortunates and is provided free lodging for the night through the efforts of a self-appointed social worker.

### Commentary

The indignity of Hurstwood's situation is made more severe by the remnants of pride that are left to him. In fact, weakened in body and mind, he seems to be in a state of chronic shock. Often he finds himself repeating out loud snatches of conversation and the tag ends of jokes he remembers from the days when he had been a successful manager in Chicago. "As the present became darker, the past grew brighter, and all that concerned it stood in relief."

The man manages to survive for a time by learning the science of face reading. Some people, he discovers, are more easily touched for handout than others. In the incident outside the theater in Chicago Hurstwood ignored a panhandler seeking money for a night's keep. It was finally the good-natured Drouet who gave the man a dime, while Hurstwood continued his animated conversation with Carrie. Now, through a series of fateful reversals, he is the panhandler.

## CHAPTER 46

### Summary

Preparing in her dressing room one evening, Carrie is disturbed by a commotion outside the door. In walks Drouet, who has just bribed the doorman. The next evening over dinner

Drouet tells Carrie about Hurstwood's theft from Fitzgerald and Moy's. She is moved to a genuine sorrow for Hurstwood, thinking that he must have done it for her sake.

Drouet had hoped to win Carrie back again, but eventually he sees that his efforts are in vain. As a matter of fact, Carrie's reticence is noticed by more people than Drouet; she has acquired a reputation among the public as a somewhat mysterious, withdrawn figure.

One night Hurstwood finally approaches Carrie outside the theater and asks for money. He is so ashamed and downtrodden that he slips away as soon as Carrie hands him the contents of her purse. Their exchange of remarks has been very brief and perfunctory.

After returning to New York from a London engagement, Carrie meets Bob Ames several times; he urges her to alter her repertoire to include more serious drama. "If I were you," he tells her, "I'd change." The effect of his remark is like "roiling helpless waters." It causes Carrie to despond in her rocking chair for several days. "It was a long way to this better thing – or seemed so – and comfort was about her; hence the inactivity and longing."

## Commentary

By parading through Carrie's new life the three major figures of her past, Dreiser succeeds in providing "closure" or completeness to the structure of the novel. One cycle has completed itself and now another begins. Carrie is able to weather the reappearance of Drouet and the news he brings of the past Chicago incident; she is able even to overcome her hostility toward Hurstwood. Carrie cannot escape unscathed, however, from the influence of Bob Ames. Believing that Ames holds a key to the future, she idolizes the man and hangs on his every word. There is, of course, a certain amount of truth in Ames' observation: "Most people are not capable of voicing their feelings. They depend upon others. That is what genius is for. One man expresses their desires for them in music; another one in poetry; another one in a play. Sometimes nature does it in a face—it makes the face representative of all desire. That's what has happended in your case." Ames further observes that Carrie will lose this quality if she persists in expressing only personal desire and neglects the desires of the rest of humanity. It is then that Carrie retires to her rocker in the attempt to root out her personal desire. She hopes to find "that better thing."

## CHAPTER 47

### Summary

Hurstwood spends his time wandering from one charity line to another. He often thinks of suicide, but usually does not have the fifteen cents required for a cell with a gas jet. Once he attempts to see Carrie backstage at the theater, but the doorman throws him out bodily. Hurstwood wanders off helplessly, crying, begging, "losing track of his thoughts, one after another, as a mind decayed is wont to do."

Carrie sits with Lola in their comfortable chambers in the Waldorf, reading *Père Goriot,* a novel about misery and suffering that Ames had prescribed for her. The night is cold and stormy, so Carrie decides to take a coach to the theater.

Drouet meets another bachelor in the lobby of another luxurious hotel. The two young men agree to invite two girls out for dinner.

Mrs. Hurstwood, her daughter Jessica, and Jessica's wealthy husband ride eastward in a Pullman somewhere between Chicago and New York. The three are headed for a holiday in Rome.

Hurstwood stands outside a Bowery flophouse waiting for the doors to open. When they do, he pays his fifteen cents, retires to his cell, locks the door, and seals the crack beneath it with his ragged overcoat. Sighing to himself, "What's the use?" he turns on the gas jet and settles down on the cot.

In her rocking chair by the window Carrie sings and dreams of the "tangle of human life." Carrie is a "harp in the wind," one of the "emotionally great" "who respond to every breath of fancy, voicing in their moods all the ebb and flow of the ideal."

## Commentary

The panoramic technique of the final chapter is used to illustrate the ebb and flow of life. Some, like Hurstwood, fall along the way. He has become part of the "class which simply floats and drifts, every wave of people washing up one, as breakers do driftwood upon a stormy shore." Some, like Carrie, rise, always grasping for the next narrow ledge, but never know the happiness of which they dream. Others, like Drouet and Hurstwood's wife and daughter, simply continue along the same dead run, never knowing what the future may bring.

> Sitting alone, [Carrie] was now an illustration of the devious ways by which one who feels, rather than reasons, may be led in the pursuit of beauty. Though often disillusioned, she was still waiting for that halcyon day when she should be led forth among dreams become real. Ames had pointed out a farther step, but on and on beyond that, if accomplished, would lie others for her. It was forever to be the pursuit of that radiance of delight which tints the distant hilltops of the world.

> Oh, Carrie, Carrie! Oh, blind strivings of the human heart! Onward, onward, it saith, and where beauty leads, there it follows....In your rocking chair, by your window dreaming, shall you long, alone. In your rocking chair, by your window, shall you dream such happiness as you may never feel.

The famous closing passage reveals Dreiser's attempt to gather together the major themes of the novel. After rendering a final glimpse of all the important characters, he turns his attention to Carrie as a representative of the universal striving of humanity. Those who "reason" can ultimately find only the sordid and the ugly. The man of reason cannot answer his own question, "What's the use?" Those who live by emotion can at least dream of an answer to their question, "Where is beauty?"

# CHARACTER ANALYSES

## CARRIE MEEBER

Carrie is the central character of the novel, but in many ways she is no ordinary protagonist. She is not notably courageous, honest, intelligent, or unselfish. She is the result of Dreiser's desire to portray "life as it is," sympathetically showing imperfect humanity in an uncertain world. Carrie has little influence over the events of the novel, and her actions and decisions are for the most part "passive." She is sent to Chicago by her parents, seduced by Drouet, and abducted by Hurstwood. She does make a crucial break from Hurstwood in New York, but by that time her fate has been decided.

Throughout the novel, Carrie is presented as "a lone figure in a tossing, thoughtless sea," and the repeated appearance of related metaphors shows Carrie to be almost without blame for her compromising morality, her adultery, and her lack of natural feeling.

Because of the conflicts within her—between "the flesh" and "the spirit," or the pursuit of pleasure and her inherited morality—Carrie is never able to make decisions and thus finds herself continually exploited by others. Although the mainstay of her character is her "desire for pleasure," Carrie possesses a deep moral sense which prevents her from acting spontaneously. This moral sense abates, however, and eventually she allows herself to ride the waves of fortune, on the lookout always for wealth and attention.

In her fantastic dreams of desire, Carrie mistakes success for happiness. The novel ends with Carrie still ignorant of her terrible mistake. A large part of Carrie's tragedy is that she is unable to feel in real life the emotions she feels onstage. Like Madame Bovary, she is unable to reconcile the world of fancy with the world of reality, and thus she is destined to remain alone, rocking in the darkness.

Carrie is, finally, a sentimental character, not a passionate one. In the melodrama of the novel, Carrie begins as the heroine of a popular romance, the naive, dreamy-eyed, ambitious but virtuous youngest sister; she emerges as a sort of nun, a "sister of the poor," dedicated to charity, lonely and celibate. Even though she undergoes very obvious outward changes and even though her life style is drastically altered, Carrie never achieves any significant insights about herself or the world at large. In this respect she remains static in a world of flux and constant change.

## CHARLES DROUET

The portrayal of Drouet is intentionally sketchy and shallow, for no subtleties or complexities of action or motivation lie beneath his flashy facade. He is generous to Carrie, but his generosity springs from his natural egotistical attempt to make Carrie a creature of his desire. Although he is good-natured and sympathetic, he is prevented from understanding Carrie by his own immaturity. While Carrie and Hurstwood learn to some extent at least that material possessions and smart appearances are false signs of a person's worth, Drouet continues to embrace the materialistic values responsible for Carrie's heartsore sadness and Hurstwood's suicide.

Drouet's function in the novel is to serve as a fixed point for measuring the changes that come over Carrie and Hurstwood. He is the first person Carrie meets when she leaves Columbia City and very nearly the last one she speaks with at the end of the novel. Ironically, it is Drouet who affects Carrie's life most drastically, planning her debut as an actress, introducing her to Hurstwood, and above all, making her aware of herself as a woman; nevertheless, Drouet himself remains unchanged and insensitive to the changes he has wrought.

# GEORGE HURSTWOOD

Hurstwood is an "ambassador" sent from the world of wealth and fashion and fine manners to Carrie's pedestrian world. Dreiser uses the character of Hurstwood to show the workings of uncertainty; for as Carrie unexpectedly rises to wealth and fame, Hurstwood loses his ability to maintain his status and gradually sinks into the depths of poverty and despair.

Because of his selfish desire to recapture his youth and find excitement at Carrie's expense, Hurstwood evokes little sympathy until the final stages of his ruination. Nevertheless, he is not willfully cruel. His fine manners and wealthy appearance show him to be very much a man of his time. He knows that his place in a carefully ordered society is well near the top, and he behaves accordingly. He believes that his attraction to Carrie will result only in a harmless flirtation that would benefit Carrie as well as himself.

Never really questioning the security of his position, he simply chooses to take the precautions necessary to guard his fine reputation. He does not wish to alter his relationship with his family or cause unfavorable publicity for his employers. He simply wants to have Carrie to himself. A complex set of circumstances and events causes him, however, to operate completely on impulse and he becomes a "man of action" for a time.

In New York, Hurstwood begins to lose the confidence and self-assurance that made him seem so hardy, dignified, and decisive. As his meager resources dwindle Hurstwood finds it impossible to obtain employment suitable to a man of his former means and position. He finds that with increasing age he is losing his vitality and drive. He bitterly resigns himself to failure, for he cannot understand the mechanics of a world that flings a man down from success to beggary. Only part of the blame rests on Hurstwood; the rest comes from the society itself, with its oppressive morality and barbaric economy.

Shortly before the final stages of his dissolution, Hurstwood evokes sympathy as never before. He is then the shadow of the man he once had been. Time and again he gathers the vestiges of his dignity and pride to search for any kind of work. His ruin is total and complete when he throws aside all his pride to work as a streetcar motorman, only to discover that even at that he is a failure.

## JULIA HURSTWOOD

Julia Hurstwood's presence in the novel enables Dreiser to construct a neat symmetry of parallels, contrasts, and conflicts among the cast of two men and two women in the novel. Drouet remains virtually unchanged after Carrie's departure; similarly, Mrs. Hurstwood continues in her self-centered ways after her divorce from Hurstwood. Also like Drouet, Mrs. Hurstwood resists change and seems to thrive on her own willfull selfishness. Thus, their futures, in contrast to those of Carrie and Hurstwood, lie safe from the vicissitudes of fortune, for they are both incapable of extending any feeling or emotion beyond their own sphere of interest. Finally they are both the jealous jilted partner in their individual domestic situations, yet they fail to place any blame upon themselves.

To the extent that his philosophy would permit it, Dreiser shows Mrs. Hurstwood to be an active agent in the shaping of events that result in the cycle of Carrie's ironic rise and Hurstwood's descent from affluent good fellow to seedy panhandler. Mrs. Hurstwood seems the very figure of doom waiting to fall upon the other main characters; she is the "villain" of the novel, the only character whose motives are purely negative. Her relationship with Hurstwood, for example, is maintained only "by force of habit, by force of conventional opinion." Because of her cold self-centeredness, she is continually frustrated, suspicious, and jealous, but her jealousy is not the product of passion, rather it is calculating and vengeful. She is aptly described as "a pythoness in humor."

In her actions and pronouncements Mrs. Hurstwood represents the upper part of the society to which she belongs. She is a moral hypocrite, eager to set adrift and forget anyone who does not conform to her narrow standards. Her values are only those of wealth, social status and appearance.

## MINOR CHARACTERS

In addition to the four central characters who have the strongest effect upon and among one another, there are several who are in various ways instrumental in shaping conditions or events in the novel or who in some way serve as parallel or contrasting figures. Carrie's sister **Minnie** is a dull prig, staid and solemnly adapted to her situation. Phlegmatic Minnie stands in opposition to all of Carrie's ambitions and dreams. As Carrie becomes more able to adapt, Drouet and eventually Hurstwood take the place of Minnie in epitomizing a fate she must avoid.

Hurstwood's children, **Jessica** and **George, Jr.**, serve as parallel figures to Carrie and Drouet. Because they had the good fortune of being born well off, however, George, Jr., and Jessica are indifferent to the plight of anyone else and are insufferably snobbish. But like Carrie they are greedy for wealth and status.

Carrie's social mentors, **Mrs. Hale** in Chicago and **Mrs. Vance** in New York, lead her to discover a host of detailed refinements concerning dress and demeanor that augment a woman's charm. They play their part in opening the girl's eyes to the decorum of those above her on the social ladder. Along with Drouet, Mrs. Hale prepares Carrie to catch Hurstwood's notice. Later on, Mrs. Vance coaches Carrie further, making her able to continue without Hurstwood.

**Lola Osborne**, eager and callow, lacks the drive or boldness to abandon herself to fortune. Unlike Carrie, Lola has taken the short route directly from home to the theater, and so she has neglected to provide herself with the "emotional greatness" that Carrie has found in life's experience. Lola replaces

Hurstwood when he is no longer fit to offer constant praise to Carrie.

**Bob Ames**, finally, combining vitality and mature wisdom, or so it seems to Carrie, serves as direct contrast to both Drouet and Hurstwood. He appeals to Carrie because he never appears to be in open pursuit of her and because he seems to have found the proper balance of personality and action. Actually, however, Ames is the third man in Carrie's life who seems to hold the key to happiness. The reader should be somewhat wary of Ames when he points out to Carrie "a farther step," the possibility of a career in straight dramatic roles instead of musicals and comedies.

## DREISER'S IDEAS AND PHILOSOPHY

Although he was to embrace Oriental mysticism as a philosophy of life in his later years, at the time he was writing *Sister Carrie* Theodore Dreiser ascribed to a "mechanistic" theory of reality. His early life impressed him with the brutality and necessity of a blind fate that imposed itself upon the weak. He came to hate ill luck and blind chance, which invariably ground to shreds any effort the common man made to raise himself. He did not rebel against fate as one rebels against evil; instead, he was so overpowered by the experiences and sights of human suffering that he saw it as a universal principle.

In the 1890's Dreiser began to read the philosophy of nineteenth-century mechanism in Darwin and Spencer, in Tyndall and Huxley. These writers afforded no new revelations but cemented and gave authority to what he had long suspected. Human life was without purpose or meaning; man is an underling, a worthless blob of protoplasm on a dying planet whirling aimlessly through space—in Dreiser's own words, "a poor, blind fool."

Hating from early childhood anything to do with religion, Dreiser found in mechanism a scientific sanction for suffering.

The theory of evolution, as it was then conceived, revealed nature as a ruthless process of the struggle for survival; this was merely an extension on a larger scale of what Dreiser had observed in his boyhood and youthful travels through the eastern United States. Untrained in logical thought, he had little trouble in transferring the theories of evolution to everyday reality. Mechanism, although it was rather more complicated than Dreiser perceived it, became his notion of "chemisms." Chemic compulsions consist of those desires and drives which are usually unconscious. Dreiser coined the term to evoke the sense of something largely out of human control. "Chemism" attempts to explain human behavior in the terms of chemical or physical science. Through chemisms Dreiser sought to explain all phenomena, organic as well as inorganic. Life is chemism, personality is chemism, emotions and needs are chemisms. Thus, Dreiser makes no distinction between the behavior of beasts, the human sex urge, or any sentiment which people agree to call higher or noble.

Materialism is simply mechanism as it appears in the human order. The world of men, like the world of indifferent nature, is a savage place where only the strongest can survive. Society is an aggregate whole of atomic underlings, each one an independent unit of force and desire, determined somehow by mechanical forces, pushing or making way for other forces as it bumps crazily along. Each individual encounters obstacles which destroy him or meets with fortuitous currents which help him toward his goal. The strong surge ahead, the weak fall back, or worse yet, become the slaves of their betters. This is "Darwinism" at its starkest.

Dreiser combines both the biological determinism of Darwin and the concept of blind fate in *Sister Carrie*. Severely handicapped by her innocence and poverty, Carrie appears to be caught in an inevitable spiral of disappointment and poverty, were it not for a series of circumstances and coincidences that lift her out of her condition. If Carrie had not met Drouet accidentally on the street after she lost her job, she would have returned home to Columbia City. If the safe door had not by unaccountable chance closed as Hurstwood stood by with his employers' money in his hands, Carrie would not have gotten to New York or become a famous actress. In such a world each one must take advantage of what little opportunity he has, even though it means abandoning or injuring others.

In the bleak world of Dreiser's philosophy, morality is a myth for assuaging the weak. It is a cynical agreement on the part of master and slave to keep the whole system of chemisms from running amuck. Dreiser also believed, however, that "life was somehow bigger and subtler, and darker than any given theory or order of life." It is through this loophole that Dreiser finds the way to write novels of life as it is.

Dreiser not only responds to his fellow man in a very immediate and sympathetic manner, but more importantly, despite the limits of his vision, he understands human beings. His understanding goes far beyond the determinism and chemisms through which he seeks to explain them. Were Dreiser unable to understand humanity in terms other than his restrictive philosophy, readers would not discover in his novels insights about other human beings which they did not have before. In short, Theodore Dreiser is a better artist than uis philosophy would allow him to be.

## SYMBOLISM

The naturalistic writer presents his theme through symbolic detail. In this way the symbolic level of the narrative is laid directly over the events and occurrences of the simple story itself. Dreiser's use of symbolic detail permeates the novel, ranging from careful descriptions of dress and adornment to descriptions of great American cities and their surroundings.

The author must make the reader aware that the details are important to the meaning. Dreiser generally accomplishes this end through a kind of "incremental repetition" of important details. Occasionally, however, he shows a lack of subtlety when he addresses his reader directly to reveal his intention.

By registering carefully Carrie's reaction to specific details, Dreiser shows her moving from her early naive optimism to her final disillusionment and despair. Carrie's sensitivity to details provides the emotional center of the novel. The most important patterns of details, in addition to clothing and money, are the theater, hotels, and restaurants. These comprise the walled and gilded city to which Carrie seeks entrance. Perhaps the most important single group of objects is the various rocking chairs upon which Carrie rides to dreamland, beginning in her sister's flat, continuing through the several rooms and apartments where she lives, and culminating in her vast suite in the Waldorf.

Dreiser's symbolism reveals the separate and distinct worlds of *Sister Carrie*. There is the realistic world of the "reasonable" mind and the imagined world of the "emotional" world, a world described in the novel as "Elf-land," "Dream Land," or "The Kingdom of Greatness." This is the world from which Hurstwood emerges as an "ambassador" to bring Carrie back with him. It is this world in which Carrie ironically becomes a citizen — "ironically" because it never seems to yield the rewards and beauty it promises. Life is a constant battle fought between the giant armies of frustration and desire.

## DREISER'S STYLE

The adjective "elephantine" has been reserved by critics exclusively to describe the style of Dreiser, "the world's worst great writer." It is generally awkward and ponderous; it lacks precision and it moves with a lumbering gait. Even Dreiser's sincerest admirers admit that his style is atrocious, his sentences chaotic, his grammar and syntax faulty. His wordiness and repetitions are at times unbearable; he has no feeling for words, no sense of diction, no ear for euphony. The following sentences from *Sister Carrie* are examples of Dreiser's writing style at its worst: "The, to Carrie, very important theatrical performance was to take place at the Avery on conditions which were to make it more noteworthy than was at first anticipated"; "They had young men of the kind whom she, since her experience with Drouet, felt above, who took them out."

Dreiser's style is, nevertheless, important to the totality of his work. It is as valid a part of his art as his creation of characters and selection of detail. If the style seems to indicate something that is muddled, commonplace, undiscerning, cheap, and shoddy, it does so for the sake of artistic accuracy. When Dreiser writes that he seeks to present "an accurate description of life as it is," he means among other things that a graceful and measured style would detract from or contradict the reality it seeks to present. The reader, like Carrie, must learn the hard lesson of undecorated truth. After reading the novel, one feels this is the way life was, *and is.*

A page of Dreiser's writing is as distinctive as a page from any other author. To Dreiser, the conscious artifice of a high style seemed to contradict his whole idea that life is something largely out of control. He relaxes his grip on the words and the pieces fall together as they may. Style itself is a model of the universe he sought to interpret and describe.

## CHAPTER TITLES

The original title of *Sister Carrie* was to have been *The Flesh and the Spirit;* this reveals the kind of symbolic pattern Dreiser had in mind. Carrie's craving for pleasure — as represented chiefly by money and clothes — shows the forces at work on the "flesh." Her wonder and awe, and her awareness of "the constant drag to something better" signify the workings of "spirit." Carrie seems to see herself in terms of this conventional division. Although she knows she has a powerful appreciation for material possession, she also realizes that she has an emotional depth quite beyond the scope of the genial but egotistical Drouet. It is this "sympathetic, impressionable nature" that attracts Hurstwood toward her.

A good many of the chapter titles enforce this division between body and spirit. The titles seem to provide a symbolic or allegorical framework for the narrative. They are, incidentally, cast in the style of popular magazine verse, and generally appear as metrical lines of eleven or twelve syllables. Dreiser seems to rely upon them to reveal his intentions. "The Lure of the Spirit: The Flesh in Pursuit" gives title to two successive chapters in which Hurstwood becomes seriously stirred by Carrie and asks her to go away with him. Dreiser continues to present Carrie as an ignorant but gradually awakening seeker after the significance of life in the chapter, "A Pilgrim, an Outlaw: The Spirit Detained." In this chapter Hurstwood has virtually kidnaped Carrie and is taking her to Canada with him. Carrie's "spirit" is once again stirred when she realizes that the unfortunate Hurstwood has failed and that she must strike out for herself in "The Spirit Awakens: New Search for the Gate."

It seems to be characteristic of the chapter titles to describe briefly a situation and indicate a possible reaction to it; thus the greatest part of them take the following form: "The Lure of the Material: Beauty Speaks for Itself," "A Glimpse Through the Gateway: Hope Lights the Eye," and "A Pet of Good Fortune: Broadway Flaunts Its Joys."

# REVIEW QUESTIONS AND THEME TOPICS

1. In what specific ways are Carrie and Hurstwood counterparts? Take into account their personalities, their desires, and their changing views on life. How does Drouet relate to them?

2. Consider how it would affect *Sister Carrie* if Dreiser's editorial intrusions were removed. In what ways are they relevant or irrelevant to the major themes?

3. Compare the use of coincidence in *Sister Carrie* with that in a novel by Dickens or Hardy.

4. Find several passages in the novel where style seems to be particularly important. Does the style ever change?

5. In what ways does Hurstwood contribute to his own downfall? How great a part does fate play?

6. Cite several passages where the season of the year relates to the action of the novel.

7. Select a scene or episode which seems extraneous to the entire action and give your reasons for regarding it as unnecessary to plot development.

8. What are Dreiser's reasons for reintroducing Drouet, Mrs. Hurstwood, Bob Ames, and Mrs. Vance near the end of the novel?

9. Compare the changes that occur in Carrie in the first half of the novel with the changes that occur in her in the second half. At what point does she seem to have the clearest understanding of herself?

10. How do the titles of the chapters form a commentary on theme and action in the novel?

11. How many different types of irony can you find in the novel?

12. Show how Dreiser makes use of both thematic and narrative foreshadowing. How do later events illuminate earlier events?

13. The novel is begun and bisected by train rides. How do the conditions that surround both train rides differ? Are there any other important train episodes?

14. Make a list of the various types of imagery which appear — the sea, the jungle, etc. — and discuss the ways in which they reveal Dreiser's philosophy.

15. Choose at random a scene or episode and use it to discuss how details are used to relate it symbolically with action.

16. Who is the central character of the novel—Carrie or Hurstwood? What are your reasons for thinking so?

17. Dreiser once confessed that the scene in which Hurstwood steals the money from the safe at the saloon was the hardest part of the novel to write. Why do you suppose it was so difficult?

18. Explain the thematic relevance of card games and games of chance in the novel.

19. Discuss the techniques and function of Dreiser's management of "compressed" and "extended" time. Why is time so important to the novel?

20. In what ways do the roles which Carrie plays in the theater form a commentary upon the themes of the novel?

## SELECTED BIBLIOGRAPHY

KAZIN, ALFRED, and CHARLES SHAPIRO (eds.). *The Stature of Theodore Dreiser*. Bloomington: Midland Books, 1965. A collection of newspaper reviews, articles, and essays on the life and work of Dreiser by Ford Madox Ford, James T. Farrell, H. L. Mencken, Sinclair Lewis, Lionel Trilling, Saul Bellow, Malcolm Cowley, and others.

GERBER, PHILIP L. *Theodore Dreiser*. New Haven, Connecticut: Twayne Publishers, Inc., 1964. The author combines biography with critical analysis, covering the full range of Dreiser's career from its humblest beginnings to the period of the bestsellers.

MATTHIESEN, F. O. *Theodore Dreiser*. New York: Dell Publishing Co., 1966. A biography valuable also as critique and cultural history.

MENCKEN, H. L. *"Sister Carrie's* History." New York *Evening Mail,* August 4, 1917.

SHAPIRO, CHARLES. *Theodore Dreiser: Our Bitter Patriot.* Carbondale: Southern Illinois University Press, 1962. The first full-length study of Dreiser's fiction. The author avoids biographical analysis and stresses Dreiser's artistic wholeness, but does not avoid assaying his crudities and flaws.

SWANBERG, W. A. *Dreiser.* New York: Charles Scribner's Sons, 1965. A full-length, thoroughly documented biography of Dreiser the man. The author makes no pretense of literary criticism, yet the book has the cumulative effect of a Dreiser novel with its totality of treatment, its triumphs and defeats, and its grotesqueries.

# NOTES

# To understand great authors, you need to read between the lines.

## Cliffs Complete Study Editions

The more you learn about the classics, the richer your enjoyment and the deeper your understanding become. These easy-to-use Complete Study editions contain everything a student or teacher needs to study works by Shakespeare or Chaucer. Each illustrated volume includes abundant biographical, historical and literary background information, including a bibliography to aid in selecting additional reading.

The three-column arrangement provides running commentary for the complete Cambridge edition of the Shakespeare plays, plus glossary entries explaining obscure Elizabethan words. The Chaucer titles contain running commentary, individual lines of the Middle English text, followed by literal translations in contemporary English, and glossaries.

## Complete Study Editions
8½ × 11

### $6⁹⁵ each

| Shakespeare | Qty. |
| --- | --- |
| 1416-5  Hamlet | |
| 1419-X  Julius Caesar | |
| 1425-4  King Henry IV, Part 1 | |
| 1422-X  King Lear | |
| 1428-9  Macbeth | |
| 1431-9  Merchant of Venice | |
| 1434-3  Othello | |
| 1438-6  Romeo and Juliet | |
| 1441-6  The Tempest | |
| 1445-9  Twelfth Night | |
| **Chaucer's Canterbury Tales** | |
| 1406-8  The Prologue | |
| 1409-2  The Wife of Bath | |

*Prices subject to change without notice.*

Available at your booksellers, or send this form with your check or money order to **Cliffs Notes, Inc., P.O. Box 80728, Lincoln, NE 68501**
**http://www.cliffs.com**

Cliffs NOTES INC.

☐ Money order  ☐ Check payable to Cliffs Notes, Inc.

☐ Visa  ☐ Mastercard  Signature _____

Card no. _____ Exp. date _____

Signature _____

Name _____

Address _____

City _____

State _____ Zip _____

# Cliffs

# Math Review
and
# Verbal Review
for
# Standardized Tests

Use your time efficiently with exactly the review material you need for standardized tests.

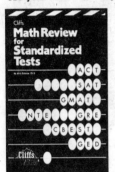

*GMAT — SAT — NTE — GRE —*
*—State Teacher Credential Tests—*
*PSAT — CBEST — ACT — PPST — GED*
*and many more!*

**Math Review** — 422 pages

- Provides insights and strategies for specific problem types, plus intensive review in the most needed basic skills in arithmetic, algebra, geometry and word problems.
- Includes hundreds of practice problems to reinforce learning at each step in a unique easy-to-use format.

**Verbal Review** — 375 pages

- Includes a grammar and usage review, dealing specifically with the concepts that exam-makers consistently use in test questions; exercises reinforce concept understanding at each step.
- Extensive practice and strategies in English usage, sentence correction, antonyms, analogies, sentence completion, reading comprehension and timed essay writing.

Cliffs Notes, Inc., P.O. Box 80728, Lincoln, NE 68501

---

Cliffs Math Review
for Standardized Tests $8.95 _____

Cliffs Verbal Review
for Standardized Tests $7.95 _____

**Cliffs NOTES**

P.O. Box 80728
Lincoln, NE 68501

- *Price subject to change without notice*

Name _____

Address_____

City _____ State _____ Zip _____

# Think Quick

Now there are more Cliffs Quick Review® titles, providing help with more introductory level courses. Use Quick Reviews to increase your understanding of fundamental principles in a given subject, as well as to prepare for quizzes, midterms and finals.

Do better in the classroom, and on papers and tests with Cliffs Quick Reviews.

**Publisher's ISBN Prefix 0-8220**

| Qty. | ISBN | Title | Price | Total | Qty. | ISBN | Title | Price | Total |
|------|------|-------|-------|-------|------|------|-------|-------|-------|
| | 5309-8 | Accounting Principles I | 9.95 | | | 5330-6 | Human Nutrition | 9.95 | |
| | 5302-0 | Algebra I | 7.95 | | | 5331-4 | Linear Algebra | 9.95 | |
| | 5303-9 | Algebra II | 9.95 | | | 5333-0 | Microbiology | 9.95 | |
| | 5300-4 | American Government | 9.95 | | | 5326-8 | Organic Chemistry I | 9.95 | |
| | 5301-2 | Anatomy & Physiology | 9.95 | | | 5335-7 | Physical Geology | 9.95 | |
| | 5304-7 | Basic Math & Pre-Algebra | 7.95 | | | 5337-3 | Physics | 7.95 | |
| | 5306-3 | Biology | 7.95 | | | 5327-6 | Psychology | 7.95 | |
| | 5312-8 | Calculus | 7.95 | | | 5349-7 | Statistics | 7.95 | |
| | 5318-7 | Chemistry | 7.95 | | | 5358-6 | Trigonometry | 7.95 | |
| | 5320-9 | Differential Equations | 9.95 | | | 5360-8 | United States History I | 7.95 | |
| | 5324-1 | Economics | 7.95 | | | 5361-6 | United States History II | 7.95 | |
| | 5329-2 | Geometry | 7.95 | | | 5367-5 | Writing Grammar, Usage, & Style | 9.95 | |

*Prices subject to change without notice.*

Available at your booksellers, or send this form with your check or money order to **Cliffs Notes, Inc., P.O. Box 80728, Lincoln, NE 68501** http://www.cliffs.com

**Cliffs NOTES** INC.

☐ Money order ☐ Check payable to Cliffs Notes, Inc.

☐ Visa ☐ Mastercard    Signature_____

Card no. _____ Exp. date _____

Name _____

Address _____

City _____ State_____ Zip_____

Telephone ( ) _____

# Legends In Their Own Time

Ancient civilization is rich with the acts of legendary figures and events. Here are three classic reference books that will help you understand the legends, myths and facts surrounding the dawn of civilization.

*Cliffs Notes on Greek Classics* and *Cliffs Notes on Roman Classics*—Guides to the idealogy, philosophy and literary influence of ancient civilization.

*Cliffs Notes on Mythology*—An introduction to the study of various civilizations as they are revealed in myths and legends.

Find these legendary books at your bookstore or order them using the form below.

## Yes! I want to add these classics to my library.

*Cliffs Notes on Greek Classics*   ISBN 0566-2 ($7.95) ................ _____

*Cliffs Notes on Roman Classics*  ISBN 1152-2 ($7.95) ................ _____

*Cliffs Notes on Mythology*         ISBN 0865-3 ($7.95) ................ _____

Total $_____

Available at your booksellers, or send this form with your check or money order to **Cliffs Notes, Inc., P.O. Box 80728, Lincoln, NE 68501** http://www.cliffs.com

☐ Money order   ☐ Check payable to Cliffs Notes, Inc.
☐ Visa   ☐ Mastercard   Signature_____

Card no. _____ Exp. date_____

Signature _____

Name _____

Address _____

City _____ State_____ Zip_____

*get the Cliffs Edge!*

**Cliffs NOTES INC.**

# Cliffs Police Examinations Preparation Guides

## Larry F. Jetmore, Ph.D.

*Written by a police professional in the time-honored tradition of "showing the way," these guides give candidates for police officer, sergeant, and management positions the edge they need for success.*

### Cliffs Police Management Examinations Preparation Guide

Prepare for promotion to several management ranks with two practice multiple-choice written exams, an essay-writing review and practice, a mock oral board with questions, a realistic assessment center, a rating of training and experience, and strategies for all.

### Cliffs Police Sergeant Examination Preparation Guide

Prepare for promotion to a supervisory position with two practice multiple-choice written exams, a mock oral board with questions, a realistic assessment center, and strategies for all.

### Cliffs Police Officer Examinations Preparation Guide

Prepare for the written, medical, physical agility, and oral board examinations and interviews with three practice 100-question written tests, a 100-question writing skills test, three physical agility tests, a mock oral board with questions, and strategies for all.

------------------------------------------------------------------------

# Cliffs Police Examinations Preparation Guides

**Publisher's ISBN Prefix 0-8220**

**ISBN**

| | | | |
|---|---|---|---|
| ☐ | 2049-1 | Cliffs Police Management Examinations Preparation Guide | $17⁹⁵ |
| ☐ | 2044-0 | Cliffs Police Sergeant Examinations Preparation Guide | $9⁹⁵ |
| ☐ | 2047-5 | Cliffs Police Officer Examinations Preparation Guide | $17⁹⁵ |

**Bill to:**                 **Ship to:**

_____     _____

_____     _____

_____     _____

**Date** _____      **Phone** _____

☐ **Visa**  ☐ **Mastercard**     **Signature** _____

**Card number** _____     **Exp. date** _____

cliffs notes, inc. • p.o. box 80728 • lincoln, nebraska 68512 • http://www.cliffs.com

# Your Guides to Successful Test Preparation.

## Cliffs Test Preparation Guides
### • Complete • Concise • Functional • In-depth

Efficient preparation means better test scores. Go with the experts and use *Cliffs Test Preparation Guides*. They focus on helping you know what to expect from each test, and their test-taking techniques have been proven in classroom programs nationwide. Recommended for individual use or as a part of a formal test preparation program.

**Publisher's ISBN Prefix 0-8220**

| Qty. | ISBN | Title | Price | Qty. | ISBN | Title | Price |
|---|---|---|---|---|---|---|---|
| | 2078-5 | ACT | 8.95 | | 2044-0 | Police Sergeant Exam | 9.95 |
| | 2069-6 | CBEST | 8.95 | | 2047-5 | Police Officer Exam | 14.95 |
| | 2056-4 | CLAST | 9.95 | | 2049-1 | Police Management Exam | 17.95 |
| | 2071-8 | ELM Review | 8.95 | | 2076-9 | Praxis I: PPST | 9.95 |
| | 2077-7 | GED | 11.95 | | 2017-3 | Praxis II: NTE Core Battery | 14.95 |
| | 2061-0 | GMAT | 9.95 | | 2074-2 | SAT* | 9.95 |
| | 2073-4 | GRE | 9.95 | | 2325-3 | SAT II* | 14.95 |
| | 2066-1 | LSAT | 9.95 | | 2072-6 | TASP | 8.95 |
| | 2046-7 | MAT | 12.95 | | 2079-3 | TOEFL w/cassettes | 29.95 |
| | 2033-5 | Math Review | 8.95 | | 2080-7 | TOEFL Adv. Prac. (w/cass.) | 24.95 |
| | 2048-3 | MSAT | 24.95 | | 2034-3 | Verbal Review | 7.95 |
| | 2020-3 | Memory Power for Exams | 5.95 | | 2043-2 | Writing Proficiency Exam | 8.95 |

*Prices subject to change without notice.*

Available at your booksellers, or send this form with your check or money order to **Cliffs Notes, Inc.,** P.O. Box 80728, Lincoln, NE 68501 http://www.cliffs.com

☐ Money order  ☐ Check payable to Cliffs Notes, Inc.

☐ Visa  ☐ Mastercard  Signature_____

Card no. _____ Exp. date_____

Signature _____

Name _____

Address _____

City _____ State_____ Zip_____

*GRE, MSAT, Praxis PPST, NTE, TOEFL and Adv. Practice are registered trademarks of ETS. SAT is a registered trademark of CEEB.